Crypto Master

The Ultimate Beginner's Guide To Cryptocurrency Trading and Investing

Frank Miller

TABLE OF CONTENTS

Introduction

Let's say you are about to make your first investment in the cryptocurrency market. Or you have invested/traded for some time but find it hard to cope with the volatility in the crypto market. You want to be well equipped for making good investing and trading decisions in one of the most promising but challenging markets – cryptocurrency.

In this book, I will go over a wide variety of elements describing how to make money in the cryptocurrency markets. With a clear, concise, and directional way of presenting all information in this book, you will have a good cornerstone to approach, understand, and benefit from this market, even if you choose a short-term or long-term investment. An interesting aspect of this book is that you will not only learn several different wonderful trading techniques, but also dig deep into money management strategies. Dozens of trade examples are available to help you gain the best understanding of the market.

Having invested in the crypto market for more than 7 years, I am proud to be a consistent, profitable trader/investor over the years. Being consistently profitable is not easy, and it takes a lot of time, patience, and practice to reach the level you dream of. This is what drives me to share with you my crypto trading techniques and experiences for the first time. I want to show people that, with serious discipline and enough care and understanding about the way we approach and deliver our decisions, trading is not that difficult.

Once you have mastered all the techniques presented in this book, you will be equipped with nearly everything you need to know about making good investment decisions and reaping profits. Good trading entails building the appropriate mindset and then acting the right way. The sooner you master your mindset and techniques, the sooner you will generate profits and avoid unnecessary (big) losses. This book is professionally designed to help you achieve all of these.

With my help and expertise, you will be ready to conquer tough challenges in the cryptocurrency market. You will not be overwhelmed by a bunch of different signals and opinions from people about what to do in each market condition. All techniques and strategies are presented in actionable steps so that a newbie can easily apply and make the best use of them. If you have traded or invested for some time without finding a profitable and reliable method, this book may fill that gap for you because this is what I have used for a long time now. Moreover, you will see how I present each strategy with a different angle to tie in with what you may know already, while keeping it simple enough to make your trading comfortable and profitable.

Unlike some other markets, the cryptocurrency market operates 24/7, meaning that traders have the chance to open and close their trades at any time. While this offers unlimited opportunities to generate benefits from market fluctuations, you may put yourself in great danger if you fail to approach and process information correctly.

Before we dive into the main part of the book, let's take a look at some of my thoughts before, during, and after writing this book.

1. Treat it as a friend of yours:

This book includes not only my strategies in trading/investing but also my thoughts and mindset about how it was cultivated through the years. There are some examples I see in the crypto metaverse that may be very familiar to you. These stories will help you avoid both mistakes as well as psychological traps that may cost you money. I hope you will treat this edition not only as a book but also as a friend who can remind you of what you should and shouldn't do.

2. Some stupid assumptions:

This is a practical book that focuses on many reliable strategies plus real examples for illustrating what I want to convey. If you are looking for a theoretical book, for instance, one about cryptocurrency and the underlying technology **described in great detail**, this may not be for you. I have tried my best to describe some angles about cryptocurrency, its development, and many relevant arsenals you need before diving into the battle. Yet, I am not sure they will meet someone's high expectations about cryptography in-depth, for example.

Moreover, please accept some stupid assumptions of mine regarding you, the reader. Are you falling into one of these groups of people?

+ You may have heard about cryptocurrency, but you don't understand how it works and how you can start investing/trading cryptocurrencies the right way.

+ Though you may have invested in other markets like the stock or forex market before, you aren't necessarily familiar with the terminology and the technical aspects of trading and investing in cryptocurrencies.

+ You have owned some cryptocurrencies, and you want to increase your profits via trading/investing, but you don't know how to do it;

+ You have certain experience in trading/investing, but you are not yet profitable.

Moreover, **I assume** that you have some basic information about candlestick patterns (e.g: What is the candlestick body? What is the candlestick shadow/wick? etc.) before buying this book. If you have no idea about candlesticks, I suggest you learn about them as well so you can understand ideas in this book better. I believe it may not take much time.

3. *This may not be exhaustive*

As you may already know, the cryptocurrency metaverse includes many aspects and these aspects are constantly changing, such as the trading fees, trading rules, incentives you may enjoy, the availability of trading platforms under geographical location, tax laws, and more.

Although I have tried to convey many different angles about the subject, you might need to investigate more to make sure you are kept updated with possible changes with regard to cryptocurrency trading and investing. Still, there is one thing that I believe will last forever: the strategies and mindset presented in this book.

Now that we have had enough greetings and getting to know each other better, let's get started with the main part of the book.

PART ONE

GET STARTED WITH CRYPTOCURRENCY

IN THIS PART

- Understanding cryptocurrencies, the huge mechanism behind them as well as big potentials as well as risks related to cryptos.

- How to prepare the best arsenals for the battles ahead.

- An in-depth discussion about how to make the most out of a bearish market;

- How to filter the best cryptos to go.

Chapter 1: Is Cryptocurrency Worth It?

Crypto At First Glance

The hype surrounding cryptocurrency has grown exponentially over the previous decade. People are increasingly looking to invest in Bitcoin and other cryptocurrencies in the hope of making some quick decent money, thanks to the wild fluctuations in this market. Whichever way you look at it, the euphoria surrounding cryptocurrency does not appear to be dying down anytime soon and Bitcoin's underlying idea is beginning to take center stage.

As more information on the blockchain, the technology that underpins Bitcoin, becomes available, the more questions people have about it. In this chapter, we will learn the basics you need to know about Bitcoin (BTC) and other cryptocurrencies, including how they work, why they exist, what the pros and cons are, how they're taxed, why you should invest in them and more.

It wasn't that long ago when the terms 'Bitcoin' and 'cryptocurrencies' became popular. Outside the crypto-communities, few people knew what they were, and many assumed they were just another craze that would fade away in a few years. One bitcoin was only worth a few bucks at that time and as a result, it was mostly overlooked by the general public.

Those who believed in cryptocurrencies were eventually rewarded handsomely, and they are still being rewarded, as a single cryptocurrency costs thousands of dollars now. For example, Bitcoin only took five years to break beyond the $1,000 barrier in late 2013. At the time of this writing, its price has surpassed the $50,000 mark! With increasing prices and rapid growth, more and more people are becoming interested in bitcoins and cryptocurrencies in general.

Bitcoin And Its Colorful History

By way of definition, cryptocurrencies are electronic versions of digital currencies. They don't exist in the same way that paper money or coins do, which you undoubtedly have in your wallet right now. You can't physically hold them, but you can use them to make purchases.

Bitcoin is not the first cryptocurrency in the world, but it is the most popular and influential among all. Other cryptocurrencies that came after Bitcoin are referred to within the crypto community as 'Alternative Coins' or Altcoins. Attempts to create digital money have been made in the past but they all failed. Why? Because the concept of virtual currencies before Bitcoin had a built-in flaw: It was easy to spend the same money twice. You could pay $100 to one merchant, send him a copy of his money which is electronic, retain the original version of that currency and then use the same amount to pay another merchant for something else! As you can imagine, scammers and con artists adored this loophole.

Then, Satoshi Nakamoto began working on the Bitcoin concept in 2007. He released his white paper "Bitcoin: A Peer-to-Peer Electronic Cash System" on 31 October of the following year, which defined a payment system that addressed the double spending problem of digital currencies. It was a wonderful concept that caught the cryptography community's attention. Just over a week after the white paper was published, the Bitcoin Project software was registered on SourceForge.net – a famous software discovery platform.

The first Bitcoin block, known as the 'Genesis block,' was mined in January 2009. Block 170 marked the first bitcoin transaction between Satoshi Nakamoto and Hal Finney (a famous American programmer) a few days later. The following year, in November 2010, the market capitalization of Bitcoin surpassed $1,000,000! This was a watershed point in the growth of Bitcoin because it prompted more individuals to get interested and invest in bitcoins. At this time, the price of one BTC was $0.50.

After reaching an all-time high of $31.91/BTC in June 2011, Bitcoin witnessed something referred to today as the "Great Bubble of 2011." The price plunged to just $10/BTC just four days after reaching its maximum point. Many investors panicked when they realized they had lost so much money and sold their remaining coins at a loss. The price took over two years to recover but it quickly surpassed the previous all-time high. The crypto value continued to move sideways during the 2014-2016 period, starting from $770 early 2014 to over $990 at the end of 2016.

It was not until 2017 that the interest in Bitcoin in particular and cryptocurrencies in general increased dramatically. Bitcoin price hovered around the $1,000 level until it broke $2,000 in May, and then surged to nearly 20,000 in late December. Mainstream investors and scientists paid strong attention to the crypto world, and more entities started developing other cryptocurrencies.

After witnessing a sharp drop in the 2018-2019 period, Bitcoin price burst into activity once again in 2020-2021 as a result of the Covid-19 pandemic. In particular, starting from $6,965.72 early 2020, the price climbed to $67,549.14 – the all time high at the time of this writing.

Those who held on to their bitcoins made the right choice, as the price has continued to rise beyond all predictions to the contrary.

What's fascinating about Bitcoin is that, while all transactions are open to the public and nothing is kept secret, no one knows who Satoshi Nakamoto is. Many believe he is a collective pseudonym for a group of cryptographic developers rather than a single person. Some have claimed to be Satoshi, but his true identity has remained a mystery to this day.

Why Have Cryptocurrencies Become More and More Popular?

Cryptocurrencies, particularly Bitcoin, were created to remedy flaws in traditional currency. To begin with, central banks and governments back our traditional currencies. As a result, they are vulnerable to corruption and manipulation, among other difficulties.

Unlike traditional currencies, Bitcoin and other cryptocurrencies are not backed by a regulatory authority, which means they are not subject to the whims of anyone. Cryptocurrencies are open-source, decentralized, and transparent. This means you can see all of the transactions that have ever taken place on the network, and you can inspect and verify the blockchain data for yourself to ensure that each transaction is genuine.

To manage the generation of new bitcoins and ensure that no double-spending occurs on the network (remember, this was the reason for the failure of the virtual currencies before Bitcoin), Bitcoin uses incredibly complicated mathematical algorithms. The result is that the Bitcoin code is so safe and advanced that it's very difficult to hack or fool the system.

Another major drawback of our traditional currency is that it does not have a finite supply. This means that governments and central banks have the power to issue more money as needed. When more money is generated and enters the market, the purchasing power of our paper money is reduced, which means we have to pay more for something we previously only paid a few dollars for. This is known as inflation.

On the other hand, the situation with Bitcoin is very different. According to the Bitcoin Protocol, only 21,000,000 bitcoins can be mined and created. This will be the total amount available, which ensures that bitcoins remain limited in supply, thus making them very precious resources.

Cryptocurrencies are also divisible, much like pennies to a dollar. A Satoshi is 1/100,000,000 of a bitcoin and is the smallest bitcoin unit. This implies that you can invest a few thousand Satoshis at a time until you have a whole bitcoin. It may take some time to get to 1 BTC if you choose this method, but if the price continues to rise, buying a few Satoshis on a regular basis may pay off in the long run.

Another reason why cryptocurrencies are gaining in popularity is because they are extremely portable, allowing you to take them with you wherever you go. Try carrying a million bucks in your briefcase or a gold backpack! It's not nearly as light as it appears in movies. With cryptocurrencies like Bitcoin, you may use a variety of digital wallets to store your money or move them around easily, allowing you to make payments whenever and wherever you desire.

In addition, regular financial policies and regulations do not apply to cryptocurrencies because they are not controlled by any centralized authority. This means you won't have to pay high bank costs that come with sending money to other people. Also, you won't have to wait several hours, if not days, for your payments to clear or post because bitcoin transactions are nearly instantaneous (usually in 10-45 minutes).

All of these advantages now lead us to exploring the cryptocurrency's underlying technology.

The Technology Behind Cryptocurrency

Bitcoin transactions look to be quick and simple on the surface, and they are. However, a big ledger known as the **blockchain** is the technology that helps the cryptocurrency network operate stably behind the scenes. It's enormous because it provides a complete record of all bitcoin transactions since the currency's release back in 2009. The blockchain will continue to expand over time as a result of increasing transactions.

Here's how it works: When you submit a payment in Bitcoins, for instance, your wallet or app sends a request to the whole Bitcoin network, which consists of computers known as nodes. These nodes then use well-known techniques to validate your transaction, which would then be joined with others to generate a new block of data for the blockchain once it has been verified and confirmed. The new block is then added to the blockchain's network and a copy of your transaction is automatically stored across the network. This is when the transaction is deemed complete and irreversible.

It might sound cumbersome but from start to completion, this procedure takes roughly 10-45 minutes (which is why Bitcoin transactions aren't instantaneous). No one can undo or erase a transaction once it has been completed. The recipient (the person to whom you transferred the bitcoin payment) will now notice your payment in his or her wallet.

Transaction Verifications

The people known as miners are the ones who verify each transaction. The bitcoin network's miners are its lifeblood. Miners have played such an important role in Bitcoin's success that they deserve to be compensated in valuable bitcoins. Aside from the block created from the Genesis block, no new blocks would have been created and added to the network without them. Transactions would not be completed if nothing is added to the blockchain. In other words, without the presence of the miners, no one on the network would have been able to send or receive bitcoin payments and no fresh bitcoins could be created.

Miners are compensated in bitcoins for their hard work because they are essential to the Bitcoin network (it would not make any sense to reward them in traditional paper currency). Seeing as there are only 21 million bitcoins for them to mine or create, the number of bitcoins that miners are paid with will continue to reduce until all bitcoins are depleted around 2140.

Bitcoin Halving

As mentioned previously, the blockchain technology that underpins Bitcoin is basically a group of computers (aka nodes) that run Bitcoin's transactions. These computers store the histories of transactions that have occurred on the blockchain network. Each complete node is responsible for accepting or rejecting one transaction in the whole network by performing various checks to verify that the transaction is genuine.

A transaction takes place only if all of the parties involved within one block concur with it. Following the approval, the transaction is added to the blockchain and broadcasted to other nodes, and the process continues. Although anyone can join the network as a node (so long as they are able to store the entire blockchain and its transaction history), not all of them are considered miners.

The blockchain becomes more stable and secure as more computers are added to it. As previously discussed, Bitcoin mining occurs when miners use their computers to process and validate transactions on the Bitcoin blockchain network. The term "mine" is employed in a very figurative sense, analogous to the process of extracting gold from the earth. After verifying transactions, the miners group them into blocks and chain these blocks together to create the blockchain.

The miners are rewarded with bitcoins when the block is filled with transactions. Now the block reward provided to Bitcoin miners for processing these transactions is cut in half every 210,000 blocks mined, or roughly every four years. As a result, the speed at which new bitcoins are released into circulation is slashed in half. Put differently, these halving events occur when Bitcoin enforces synthetic price inflation until all the coins are released into circulation.

This system is going to be in place until the year 2140. At that point, it's predicted that miners' fees would then be paid by the users of the network. These fees make sure that miners are still motivated to mine and maintain the network.

At the time of writing, there are about 18.85 million bitcoins in circulation and that leaves us with only about 2.15 million bitcoins left to be mined. Bitcoin halving is of great significance because it represents a reduction in the rate of a new Bitcoin created when the general quantity of bitcoins comes close to the maximum limit.

The reward for every block produced in the chain was 50 bitcoins in 2009. It was 25 bitcoins per block after the primary halving, then 12.5, and at last 6.25 bitcoins per block as of 11 May 2020. By comparison, consider what would happen if the quantity of gold taken from the planet was cut in half every four years. It would get even more scarce and as a result, its value may shoot up.

Bearing this in mind, what are the implications of bitcoin halving on its price and value? Well, although the demand for bitcoin is generally on a rise, these halvings diminish the speed at which new coins are minted, lowering the potential number of bitcoins in circulation. This has consequences for investors and traders alike because, once a valuable asset is scarce, limited, or in finite supply, such an asset experiences tremendous demand, pushing the price higher.

In the past, Bitcoin halvings were related to huge price increases. The first halving took place on 28 November 2012, witnessing an increase from $12 to $1,217 on 28 November 2013. The second one happened on 9 July 2016, raising the price from $647 to approximately $19,800 on 17 December 2017. Over a year, the price decreased from this top to around $3,276 on 17 Dec 2018, being 506 percent higher than the pre-halving level.

The most recent halving (based on this time of writing) took place on 11 May 2020 and at that time, Bitcoin was worth $8,787. This figure rose to $64,507 on 14 April 2021, an astonishing 634 percent increase from its pre-halving price. A month later, on 11 May 2021, bitcoin's price was $54,276, a 517 percent increase that appears to be similar to the 2016 halving's performance.

Generally, the halving chain of effects goes like this: halved reward → halved inflation → lower supply available → higher demand → higher price. Miners' incentives won't be affected regardless of the reward being cut, because Bitcoin is more valuable throughout the process.

For their part, miners would have little to no incentive if the halving process fails to raise demand and Bitcoin's price. The reward for completing transactions would be lower, and Bitcoin's value would not be attractive enough. To tackle this, Bitcoin already has an embedded program embedded in its system that will make the mining process easier. Put differently, in case the miners' reward has been cut in half while the Bitcoin value failed to rise, there would be a corresponding reduction in the degree of mining efforts required for each transaction. This serves to keep miners incentivized in the process.

This method has proven to be effective for a few times now. So far, these halvings resulted in a price spike followed by a dramatic drop. The crashes that followed these advances, however, were still able to keep prices higher than they were before the halving events. For instance, during the late 2017 – early 2018 bubble, the bitcoin value skyrocketed to around $20,000 before it plunged to approximately $3,200. This is a huge decline, but bitcoin was just about $650 before halving.

Though this strategy has worked recently, the halves are usually accompanied by a lot of hype, speculation, and volatility, and the market's reaction to these occurrences in the future is hard to predict.

How Crypto Revolutionized Our Lives

Why do we need to explore additional stores of value and means of exchange if we already have traditional money like the fiat (government-backed currency) we know today? Why should we consider using cryptocurrency? Some individuals are opposed to the use of digital currencies, but there are also ones who are in favor of adoption due to the numerous benefits of cryptocurrencies. Here are a few examples:

- Easier access to the financial system.

According to the World Bank, nearly 1.7 billion adults do not have access to financial services provided by banks. When it comes to banking services, Asian and African countries are among the worst affected. There are nearly 200 million people in China who do not yet have a bank account.

People who do not have access to banks are at risk of losing their income and assets due to natural catastrophes and calamities, as well as suffering from human issues such as theft and robbery. These people are also denied the opportunities of investment, credit, or business growth resulting from the lack of financial service access provided by organizations.

Since more individuals have access to the internet than banks, it would be much easier to sell cryptocurrencies to the unbanked. If the unbanked are given equal access to financial systems, poverty could be reduced globally.

- Individual Ownership Assurance

Looking at the existing status of financial institutions, traditional account holders can choose to allow banks to manage their assets. When banking institutions have a lot of influence on account holders' assets, this puts the holders in great danger, even if they don't realize it. On the contrary, with crypto, you can easily take full control of your asset ownership because cryptocurrencies do not rely on any centralized authority, such as a bank. You become the sole owner of your digital assets as well as the private and public encryption keys that together form your cryptocurrency network address.

The blockchain technology that backs the cryptocurrency system also provides more privacy and security. The necessary operational policies are hardcoded in the network. They can't be changed to fit the agendas of bankers, government agencies, and other financial institutions.

- Reliable Defence Against Fraudulent Transactions

When you use your credit card to pay a merchant, you must trust that the correct amount will be deducted from your account and that your personal information will not be retained intentionally for illegal purposes. Even if you're only paying for a cup of coffee, paying with a credit card allows retailers to access your whole credit line.

Whereas, the bitcoin holder can transfer exactly what he or she wants to a receiver without providing any other information. In this way, identity theft would no longer be a possibility. Moreover, because cryptocurrencies rely on a strong encryption approach similar to that employed in blockchain technology, user safety and fund security will become a lot more critical than they are with our traditional currencies.

Do Not Underestimate The Risks

The risks associated with cryptocurrencies have been a popular topic in the financial world for some time, but the economic instability that has accompanied the Covid-19 outbreak has thrown the subject into overdrive. For instance, Bitcoin reached an all-time high of more than $68,000 on 10 November 2021. While the price increase has been beneficial to those who have invested, it does not imply that Bitcoin is the safest trading or investing environment for everyone.

While some investors may continue to prosper, others, particularly those who enter now, may face substantial losses. The following are the most significant dangers associated with cryptocurrency holding and investing.

- Cryptocurrency isn't a universally accepted payment medium yet.

Unlike our traditional currencies which derive their legitimacy from the authority of our governments, cryptocurrencies are not backed by any such power. This increases the associated risks because a cryptocurrency has value only when the people who use it believe this to be true. If the market decides it's no longer valuable, it can turn into a very dangerous investment quickly.

You can lose your coins if you lose your keys.

Cryptocurrency developers set out to construct completely untraceable source codes with very powerful hacking defenses. To achieve this, they utilized impenetrable authentication processes but the unintended consequence of this is that data losses can result in financial losses. Putting money in cryptocurrency, rather than actual cash or bank vaults, is quite safe. However, if a user loses their wallet's private keys, there would be no way to recover them. Such a user would be unable to access his or her coins and would most likely suffer financial losses as a consequence.

- Adverse effects on the environment.

Mining cryptocurrencies is known to be detrimental to the environment because it requires a lot of power input, especially electricity. Bitcoin is the cryptocurrency that requires the most energy among all, which can only be processed via advanced computers. The mining processes in some countries such as China are done with coal, which causes negative effects on the environment. The use of fossil fuels like coal has raised China's carbon footprint dramatically over the past years.

- Vulnerability to Cyber-attacks

While cryptocurrencies are extremely safe, crypto exchanges sometimes are not as secure. Some exchanges save user wallet info to make it easier for their users to correctly operate their wallets and accounts. Experienced hackers could steal this information, and when they do, they would gain access to the funds.

These hackers can quickly move funds from those accounts once they have gained access. Some exchanges, Bitfinex and Mt Gox for instance, have been hacked in recent years, and Bitcoin worth hundreds to millions of dollars has been stolen. Although most exchanges are now quite secure, another breach is always a possibility.

- High Volatility.

Generally, all cryptocurrencies in supply today are founded on a relatively new idea and market. Its "fundamentals" are still being developed and understood. In comparison with traditional investment options, crypto prices are extremely volatile. The price of Bitcoin, for instance, has been known to change without warning within a day, sometimes in a matter of minutes. This makes crypto holding and trading/investing quite risky.

For example, in December 2017, Bitcoin reached a high of nearly $20,000 for the first time. That might sound appealing and Bitcoin was expected to increase even more, but just a few months later, in February 2018, the price plummeted to under $7,000. This type of dramatic decrease is likely to happen again.

Invest In Crypto? Here is Why

Now, let's come to cryptocurrency trading/ investing. Even though cryptocurrency has been available for more than 10 years (at the time of writing), some individuals are still hesitant to invest in it. "Is it too late to begin?" is probably the common question people have before entering the cryptocurrency market.

To begin with, investing in cryptocurrency is never too late. The cryptocurrency sector is steadily increasing in value as the days go by and there is still a lot of returns to be made from the market. Over time, the number of new cryptocurrencies expands, as do your alternatives. Every day, a large number of people are drawn to the market by different factors/reasons.

Let's discuss some of the most compelling reasons why you should invest in cryptocurrency below:

• High Liquidity

"Liquidity" in the cryptocurrency context refers to the ability of a digital coin to be easily converted into cash or other cryptocurrencies. Even if you have the most valuable product in your backpack, finding a buyer will be difficult if, for instance, you're stuck on a lonely island. This is why, when it comes to financial assets, liquidity is crucial.

Over the last several years, the rate of cryptocurrencies has been continuously increasing. Bitcoin and Ethereum, two of the most popular cryptocurrencies, have consistently shown positive returns. If you want to buy $100 of Bitcoins today, as long as you are connected to the internet, you may do so almost instantaneously and without any hindrance. Online crypto investment and trading grew significantly during COVID-19 when people were quarantined in their homes. As a result, the liquidity of cryptocurrencies substantially increased.

- Flexibility and independence

The crypto market is decentralized and self-contained. At the moment, no jurisdiction in the world has the ability to regulate cryptocurrency transactions. It's a stand-alone investment platform that allows users complete control over their transactions. You can convert your assets with reduced costs and commissions if you buy and sell your cryptocurrencies on an appropriate exchange.

- Unlimited Possibilities

Just like what is tenable in any other industry, when it comes to cryptocurrency investing or trading, it is important to have a large enough number of options. Currently, there are thousands of cryptocurrencies available and you have the option of investing in any of them. The top ten or twenty cryptocurrencies are preferred by most investors, but you can look at many more. A rule of thumb is to make a list of the top five cryptocurrencies after reviewing all of the essential coins and don't limit yourself to buying just one. When it comes to investing in cryptocurrency, diversification is crucial (more about that at the end of the book).

- Crypto's Future

The main reason to invest in cryptocurrencies is that they have a promising future. More and more cryptos have been introduced with various real uses by strong technical teams. Traditional finance is believed to be disrupted by cryptocurrencies in many aspects.

Every day, new strides are made in the field of cryptography and there are regular updates made as well. Efforts to create newer cryptocurrencies are also constantly made to improve the existing decentralized networks.

- The Impact of Businesses

Many large businesses and sectors are beginning to invest in cryptocurrency and use it to make payments. As a result, this gives the crypto market a boost and helps expand it even more. Wall Street, for instance, has entered the crypto realm, recognizing it as a legitimate and efficient method of payment. More than 50 of the top world businesses have begun to operate with cryptocurrency. The adoption of crypto by these powerful companies plays a vital role in the global expansion of the industry.

Many of us feel like we need to keep up with the rest of the world. Within our context here, this means keeping up with the latest technological advancements across the globe. Many people want to invest in cryptocurrency but are afraid to take the very first initial steps. If you're one of them, don't worry. After you've grasped the principles from this book, you'll be fine.

Crypto Taxation

Due to crypto's decentralized and anonymous character, governments all over the world have struggled to find a way to allow for crypto's lawful use, but also consider any tax implications, and deter illegal activity. The result is that cryptocurrency is regarded as an asset, not a currency, in the USA and some other countries around the world. It is outrightly outlawed in some countries (China, Russia) while also being acknowledged in others. By the time of this writing, Japan is the only government in the world to recognize cryptocurrency as a currency, and its crypto regulations are the most lenient.

The legal definition of cryptocurrency in a country, as well as the tax structure in place, have a big impact on how crypto is taxed around the world. Some countries impose a Wealth Tax instead of Capital Gains Tax (CGT), while others impose both Income Tax and CGT. Some countries impose either Income Tax or CGT, but no Wealth Tax. Let's briefly discuss how cryptocurrency's tax laws differ among countries.

- The United States

Cryptocurrency is regarded as an asset (not currency) in the United States, and as such when sold, it is subject to CGT. The cost basis of a crypto asset is the price paid when it is purchased. The price at which the crypto asset is disposed of is its selling price. The difference between these two prices is the capital gains. Furthermore, where the crypto asset was not held up to a year, any profits or losses accruing from such asset would be taxed at the highest marginal rate that applies to your taxable income. The tax rate can be substantially lower when the crypto asset was held longer than one year.

- Australia

Crypto assets are generally subject to CGT in Australia, just like they are in the United States since the country views them as assets.

- The United Kingdom.

Cryptocurrency assets are treated as personal investments in the UK, but depending on the transaction they may also be taxed under CGT when being sold. In a situation where an individual runs a business that trades crypto assets, when trading profits are realized, income tax laws take precedence over CGT.

- Canada

In Canada, crypto trading is subject to either the CGT or income tax, depending on the transaction type. If income comes from a business, the entire amount is taxed, however when treated within CGT rules, only 50% of the amount is taxed.

- The Netherlands

The Netherlands utilizes a Wealth Tax and does not tax capital gains. With some exclusions, after liabilities at the beginning of each tax year are deducted from the value of the asset, the Wealth Tax is imposed at a flat interest of 31% at the time of this writing.

- Germany

Germany recognizes cryptocurrency as private money and so crypto profits are tax-free if they are less than 600 Euros a year.

- Finland

In Finland, the Supreme Court has determined that virtual currencies should be treated as assets rather than liabilities. Put differently, the capital gains tax will apply.

As you can see, the taxation of crypto varies from country to country. This means that owning cryptocurrencies may result in income tax, capital gains tax, or wealth tax, depending on the nation where you normally reside.

Crypto Jargons: Ok, You Will Become Familiar With Them

Have you ever come across a slew of cryptocurrency words and found yourself wondering what they mean? Crypto slang and jargon may be frightening, but don't worry, they will become clearer and easier to remember as time goes on. Many of the terminologies used in the crypto community originated from the gaming world but some others were coined from random phrases that have become popular among crypto users. In this section, we'll discuss some of the most popular cryptocurrency phrases and their meanings. If you are already familiar with basic crypto terminologies, you may skip this section.

- DApps

This is short for "Decentralized Applications". DApps are programs, not controlled by any central authority, that run on top of the blockchain.

- Wallet

A wallet is a virtual space where users store their cryptocurrencies to keep them safe. This is one of the most commonly used cryptocurrency terminologies and we will discuss the topic in greater detail in the next chapter.

- Address

A crypto address is a form of identification consisting of alphanumeric characters that indicate the location to which cryptocurrency will be transmitted.

- Public keys

Your public key is the set of cryptographic characters you can give out to others to enable them to send you some cryptocurrency.

- Private keys

This is how you get into your wallet, which is where you keep your cryptocurrency. Your private keys should only be accessible by you. If they fall into the wrong hands, your funds could be stolen.

- Cold Storage

This is when people keep their secret keys off the Internet and away from prying eyes.

- Hardware Wallets

A wallet is a small physical item that is used to store money. Hardware wallets are the most secure way to save your cryptocurrency.

- Token

A token is the cryptocurrency's underlying digital asset that may be used to make transactions or pay for services. Tokens are also known as coins.

- Satoshi

A Satoshi or SAT is the smallest Bitcoin denomination, equal to one hundred billionths of a Bitcoin. Satoshi Nakamoto, the developer of Bitcoin, was the inspiration for the name.

- Exchange

People can go to crypto exchanges to buy, sell, or trade cryptocurrencies.

- Hash

Refers to information decryption. To mine cryptocurrency blocks, miners must decipher hashes. You can mine more blocks and collect more block rewards if you have more hashing power.

- 51% attack

A cyberattack in which a hacker can execute double-spends and other nefarious behaviors if he or she gains 51 percent of the hashing power. Such an attack would very certainly lead to the demise of a cryptocurrency.

- Stablecoin

A cryptocurrency that is said to be linked to the value of another currency, such as the US dollar, to make it more stable and less volatile in price swings.

- Private coins

A cryptocurrency with the ability to make transactions private. Monero, Dash, and Zcash are three of the most well-known privacy coins.

- Utility Coin

Apart from transactions, it's a cryptocurrency that may be used for other things. Binance Coin, for example, can be used to gain a discount when buying other coins on the Binance exchange.

- Pump and dump

This is a scam in which people - usually the developers of the cryptocurrency who possess a major percentage - encourage others to acquire their cryptocurrency to artificially inflate the price. When the price hits a level that the scammers are happy with, they sell all they own, causing the price to drop.

- Bagholder

This cryptocurrency word refers to someone who holds onto his or her coins for such an extended time frame that the coins lose their value. This could happen after a pump and dump, for instance.

- Rekt

This is a slang term for 'wrecked.' It means the person has lost a significant amount of money on cryptocurrency.

- Moon

When a cryptocurrency is said to be "heading to the moon," it signifies that people expect its value will skyrocket.

- HODL

This is an intentional misspelling of the word 'hold' which has caught on in the crypto community. People now use it to express their intention to wait and hold a coin.

- A Whale (or Crypto Whale)

A whale is a cryptocurrency trader who can shift massive quantities of cryptocurrency in a single transaction. This has the potential to have a significant impact on the market.

- Goxxed

When a user leaves their bitcoin on an exchange and is subsequently hacked and loses all of their funds.

- DAO

The acronym DAO stands for 'Decentralized Autonomous Organisation' - a group of developers and shareholders who vote on how the blockchain should develop.

- Gas

A cost that is charged for validating a transaction. This word is most commonly associated with Ethereum blockchain based cryptocurrency.

- Node

A machine or computer that contributes to the decentralization of the blockchain network.

- Consensus

A consensus in cryptocurrency refers to when there is agreement on the blockchain about what has happened, such as transactions. If there is no consensus, it is possible that an attack has occurred or that the blockchain is vulnerable to attack.

- ICO

This stands for 'Initial Coin Offering,' which is when a new cryptocurrency offers discounted coins in exchange for another cryptocurrency, such as Bitcoin. ICO's main purpose is to fund the project.

- White paper

A white paper is a document that explains what a cryptocurrency is designed to accomplish and how it will do it. Satoshi Nakamoto published the first Bitcoin white paper. Almost every cryptocurrency has issued one since then.

- Immutable

This term is frequently used to describe distributed ledgers as found in the blockchain. Such ledgers cannot be changed, in other words, they are immutable. You cannot remove information or a transaction stored on them once such details have been entered.

- Fungible (or fungibility)

This refers to whether or not something can be swapped out for another. If a coin is fungible in bitcoin, it should have the same value everywhere.

- Proof of Work (PoW)

This is one of the most widely used cryptographic techniques. It is a system that requires miners to show proof of their work in the blocks in order to qualify for block rewards.

- Proof of Stake (PoS)

This is a widely used method that requires users to stake some of their money for transactions to be validated. This approach, according to some, is far more efficient than Proof of Work.

- Hard Fork

A hard fork is a major change to the blockchain that forces an upgrade to the network. It can validate unvalidated blocks as well as invalidate validated ones. More importantly though, when a hard fork occurs, a new cryptocurrency is typically created as a consequence.

- Soft Fork

An update to the blockchain technology that is backward compatible. They're not as severe as hard forks.

There are several other slang and crypto jargons but for our purposes, the above-listed ones will serve. The crypto market is ever-growing and once you begin, you will learn and master more of these slang terms quicker than you imagine.

Chapter 2: Geared Up For Battle

Now you might have a good understanding of how cryptocurrencies work and how they can revolutionize our lives in many ways. In this chapter, we will learn about necessary elements in crypto trading that you should understand and keep in mind all the time. Imagine the crypto market as a battle, where you have to equip yourself with different arsenals before stepping onto the battlefield. We will learn how to buy and store cryptocurrencies and what crypto exchanges are. We will also discuss trading leverage as well as showing in great detail every element in trade execution and how to trade on one big crypto exchange at the end of the chapter. Now, let's get started.

Crypto Wallets: The Keys

A crypto wallet works similarly to a physical wallet in that it stores your payment instruments. You can think of your crypto wallet as your regular keychain where multiple pairs of private and public keys are stored (with new public keys being generated with each new transaction). These keys allow you to receive, store, and transmit cryptocurrency to other users, as well as check the balance of your cryptocurrency wallet.

As far as wallets go, there are two major types: hot and cold wallets/storage. Hot wallets are internet-connected, making them less secure and more vulnerable to hacks but more convenient for everyday transactions. A good example of this type is a web wallet. Conversely, a cold wallet is more secure because users' information is stored offline, causing much less vulnerability from malware or viruses. A typical example of this is a hardware wallet.

Before discovering some types of cryptocurrency wallets you should consider using, let's first go over some features of using the wallets.

Some features to look for when choosing a Crypto Wallet

The blockchain stores all of the information about your transfers and deposits. As a result, it's critical to choose a wallet that has a strong security system. You must safeguard your wallet against thieves breaking into your passcodes and gaining access to the wallet. Most digital wallets are password-protected, and many of them have additional layers of security like encryption or two-factor authentication, among others.

Also, you need to make sure that your wallet matches the cryptocurrency you're using it for. Every cryptocurrency has a wallet it is most compatible with and you should pay attention to this. If you don't, you risk setting up a wallet that might not effectively store all your crypto assets. Put differently, you might end up losing your money.

Lastly, for the purposes of depositing and withdrawing your cryptocurrency, you need to ensure that your wallet doesn't impose any hidden fees or other superfluous expenses. While most of these fees are small, depending on the volume of your transactions, they can quickly pile up and cost you a lot of money.

How To Move Crypto Assets From Your Wallet

Transferring crypto is simple, for the most part. The actual procedure for moving each cryptocurrency can vary from wallet to wallet but there are a few constants. For instance, to transfer your cryptocurrency regardless of your type of wallet, you'll always need to know the recipient's address.

Your recipient address will be a long alphanumeric string of digits and letters that will be supplied to you after being generated by the blockchain network at random. You may either copy and paste this address key to make your transfer or use a QR code instead. You'll need to follow your other transfer instructions provided by your wallet provider closely as well.

How long does it take to send cryptocurrency from one wallet to another?

For the most part, cryptocurrency transfers are usually accomplished in a matter of minutes. Still, there are a few situations when the transfer is delayed, and it may take days for the transfer to complete. A delay can be caused either by an unexpected barrier within the blockchain, or a low order transaction cost.

If a delay occurs, the only option is to be patient and wait for the transfer to complete, as changing the transfer cost once the process has begun is impossible. The blockchain may occasionally cancel a transaction, in which case all money is promptly returned to the sender.

Confirm a transfer of cryptocurrencies

You should receive notification that the transfer was successful once it is completed. If this doesn't happen, you can double-check your transaction by looking up the recipient's address. You can do this through the following steps:

- Open a blockchain explorer website such as blockchain.com, BlockCypher, or Block Explorer.

- Search for your recipient's address.

- Select the transaction that corresponds to the Bitcoin amount you're anticipating. You may also look up the transaction's date of completion.

- Once the above has been done, you can view the full specifics of the transactions on the date you made the transfer. If the details do not correspond with your transfer, then there might have been a delay as explained above.

How to fund your Cryptocurrency Wallet

You can either find a certified vendor or use an ATM (in the case of Bitcoin) to accomplish this. If you choose to work with a vendor, you must take further steps to ensure that the vendor is legitimate and certified. You should also double-check your address to ensure it is correct.

A Bitcoin ATM is an internet-connected kiosk where consumers may buy Bitcoin and transfer it to their digital wallets in return for cash. To avoid being robbed when depositing your money, use a Bitcoin ATM in a safe and secure neighborhood, just as you would with any big deposit. Another thing to keep in mind is that certain Bitcoin ATMs have transaction limits, so if you want to make a large deposit, you might be better off splitting it up over a few days.

How to keep your wallet safe

Your wallet is where you store all the keys to your crypto assets and as a result, it's critical to take measures to keep your wallet safe. Here are a few suggestions for this:

• Anonymity

To receive transfers, wallet users must usually prove their identity, therefore addresses and wallets are never completely anonymous. When selecting your crypto wallet, look for the best security features to ensure that your wallet is as secure as possible. Also, keep your addresses private and never give them out to anyone you don't know.

• Keys and Privacy

Each crypto wallet has two sorts of keys: a public and a private key. These keys are a pair, and you'll need them to access your assets and exchange cryptocurrency. The public key makes it possible for you to receive money from others while the private key gives you access to all the crypto assets in your account. You should offer the receiver a public key and guard the private key very seriously. Without your private key, you may never access the crypto assets you have received.

To protect users' anonymity, many wallets generate a new public key each time they send money. In this way, using public keys can enhance your security and privacy drastically.

How to Withdraw from Your Wallet

The withdrawal process varies slightly among crypto wallets, therefore the methods to cash out depend on whatever wallet you use. Nonetheless, the majority of them adhere to the following guidelines:

- To begin, locate the send/receive button and navigate to that page.

- Next, connect and unlock your ledger after you've reached the send/receive page.

- Then, recheck the address that appears on your device. Make sure the address is yours, not from anyone else.

- The ledger will give you the option to copy the address or generate a QR code. Use these options because copying the address by hand may result in serious errors.

Again, be absolutely certain that the wallet address to which you're sending your cryptocurrency is correct. There is no way to retrieve your money if you accidentally send it to the wrong address. For Bitcoin, you can also use a Bitcoin ATM, though moving large amounts of cash from an ATM to your car, especially in a hazardous zone, can be risky.

Also, because most wallets charge fees for cashing out, you'll want to plan ahead of time how much you'll cash out. Coinbase, for example, charges 4% on each transaction. These kinds of costs can mount up over time. You may also have to pay taxes on any profit you make from your coins, depending on your country, as discussed in the previous chapters. Before making continuous transfers to maximize your savings, make sure you understand the fees and taxes you'll have to pay.

Bitcoin Wallets To Choose From

As discussed earlier in this section, there are several types of crypto wallets currently. Let's take a look at the four most popular representatives below:

- Mobile Wallets

A mobile wallet is a wallet that you use on your phone to manage your crypto assets and make your transactions, among other things. The ease of using mobile wallets is unrivaled. They work in the same manner as Apple Pay or any other mobile payment system, allowing you to pay for things in stores that allow cryptocurrency.

A mobile wallet may be ideal for you if you plan on spending your crypto assets rather than saving or investing them. However, if you opt for this type of wallet, all of your crypto information would be saved on your phone. You must therefore take great care of your phone because if you lose it, any experienced hacker can hack into and steal your data and assets. Furthermore, because your phone connects to the internet, if you opt for a mobile wallet, your chances of catching a virus or malware could be quite high.

In short, if you put enough attention to security and device protection, mobile wallets could be a good option to ensure quick and convenient transactions.

Among the most popular mobile wallets are Bitcoin Wallet, Blockstream, Mycelium, BitPay.

- Hardware Wallets

A hardware wallet is the best option if you want maximum security. This is derived from the fact that this cold wallet stores users' keys and data on a separate device (akin to a USB drive) that is not linked to the internet. Users can still make online transactions with hardware wallets, giving you the same ease of a hot wallet with an added layer of security from the offline storage function.

The only downside is that this security often comes at a high cost. While there are probably less expensive wallets available, hardware wallets can cost as much as $150 per device. Yet, if you put asset protection on top priority, this type of wallet is definitely the best option.

Among the most popular hardware wallets are Ledger Nano X, Trezor One, SafePal S1.

- Desktop Wallets

As the name implies, a desktop wallet operates on your desktop computer, and you store all of your cryptocurrencies on the computer.

With this type of wallet, you have full control over your money. However, because your computer is connected to the internet when it's in use, it is susceptible to viruses and malware, which can put the wallet in danger. Hence, it is highly recommended you choose a secure enough password and a verification method to prevent the wallets from dangers in the online environment.

Some popular desktop wallets include Atomic Wallet, BitPay, Electrum.

- Web Wallets

Web wallets offer a convenient middle ground between desktop and mobile ones. They are online crypto wallets that you can use on your desktop or on the go, giving you maximum flexibility and convenience. This type of wallet is also useful in the event of a hardware malfunction or when you misplace your phone.

However, web wallets do not provide the same level of control compared to a typical desktop or mobile wallet. Lastly, because it is still Internet-connected, you need to equip this type of wallet with a strong enough backup method to prevent it from online hackers.

Robinhood is a typical representative of this type of wallet.

Which Is the Best Option?

The first step here is to figure out what you want to use your crypto wallet for. You can narrow down your search once you've decided what your exact requirements are.

What are your crypto needs? Will you use it primarily to transfer crypto to cash? If this is the case, you should look for a wallet with cheap transfer costs. If you focus on storing huge sums of money in your wallet, you should use a cold wallet to ensure that it is protected as much as possible. If you're just getting started and you only have a little money to spare for crypto, a hot wallet might be a better choice because it's more convenient to use on the road and often costs less than a cold wallet.

Finally, ensure your wallet is compatible with your computer and phone (i.e., if you use Apple, make sure your wallet works well with Apple devices). Whatever wallet you choose, make sure you do your homework first, primarily to make sure the service didn't suffer hacking attacks in the past and whether they offer a product that's secure overall.

Now that you know a bit more about your crypto wallet, let's discuss where you can buy your cryptocurrency.

Crypto Sellers: Where To Look For Them

Cryptocurrency can be purchased from other users, exchanges, and stockbrokers. All cryptocurrencies are generally subject to higher volatility than many traditional assets. Hence, one rule of thumb is to allocate no more than 10% of your portfolio with any risky assets such as Bitcoin. Before you commit your funds to any cryptocurrency, here are a few things you need to know:

- Have the information you would need on hand.

Setting up your crypto account will only take a few minutes but depending on your seller, you might need to provide personal details like your Social Security number, your bank account details, a valid photo ID, and your debit or credit cards to fund your account. Remember to keep track of any new passwords you create for your crypto account or crypto wallet carefully.

- Credit cards or not?

While some providers accept a credit card for crypto payment, investing with a high-interest card like this should be carefully considered.

- Study any Investor Protections Documents supplied to you.

If any investor protection documents are provided by the platform, it's important that you study and fully understand them. The Securities Investor Protection Corporation does not protect Bitcoin and other cryptocurrency investments from exchange failures or theft, although regular stock brokerage accounts are covered up to $500,000. Some sellers offer private insurance up to a certain amount while some take care of other types of internet breaches. The more information you have here, the better your decisions will be.

- Make sure you're connected to the internet over a secure, private connection.

This is critical whenever you conduct financial transactions over the internet. Make sure that your connection is private, password-protected, and secure.

Below are some steps in buying Bitcoin:

1. Decide where you'll get your bitcoins.

- Cryptocurrency exchanges

Exchanges are the top option for your cryptocurrency purchasing purposes. As we progress through this chapter, we'll talk about exchanges. For now, let's move to other methods.

- Traditional brokers

At the time of this writing, there are not many options for purchasing and selling cryptocurrencies from traditional brokers. Robinhood was the first prominent investment broker to offer such services (this broker is available in most, but not all, U.S. states). One advantage of this platform is it doesn't apply fees in connection with bitcoin trades.

- Other ways to purchase cryptocurrencies

- Bitcoin ATMs.

These ATMs operate similar to the traditional ones. They only differ in that you can use them to purchase and sell bitcoin. There are more than 27,000 bitcoin ATMs in the United States, according to Coin ATM Radar.

- From Cryptocurrency Owners.

Peer-to-peer platforms such as LocalBitcoins com, Bisq, and Bitquick can give you direct access to the crypto owners you wish to buy from. If you're opting for this route, please proceed with great caution, ideally with people you know.

- ETFs (exchange-traded funds)

These are a type of mutual funds that you can also buy cryptocurrency from. In October of 2021, ProShares, a financial corporation, released the first Bitcoin ETF. Yet, the fund (ticker: BITO) does not invest directly in bitcoins; but rather in Bitcoin futures contracts.

- Grayscale Investments

Grayscale Investments is a firm that manages cryptocurrency assets. Grayscale Bitcoin Trust (GBTC) and Grayscale Ethereum Classic Trust (ETCG) are two of its investment trusts that are openly listed, which means you may buy them from a variety of discount brokers.

2. Decide how you'll keep your bitcoins

As previously discussed, there are several types of crypto wallets available for your needs. Go through these options carefully and depending on your needs, make the choice appropriate for you. Whichever wallet you choose, make sure that it is secure enough for transactions.

3. Confirm your purchase

After you've linked your crypto wallet to your preferred seller, the next step is perhaps the simplest: selecting how much cryptocurrency you wish to buy. While one bitcoin can cost thousands or even tens of thousands of dollars, you can buy and sell it in smaller fractions. With that, purchasing crypto has become easier than ever.

Now, let's discuss Crypto exchanges and how they work.

Crypto Exchanges: Where You Show Your Best Performances.

A cryptocurrency exchange functions similarly to a traditional online brokerage. The basic difference is specialization: Traditional brokers specialize in securities and other regular financial instruments, whereas crypto exchanges cater solely to crypto investors. Furthermore, several of these exchanges provide additional investing possibilities.

Most exchanges provide custody and storage services for their users to keep their crypto assets safe from cyber theft. They also make it easy to transfer your money from your exchange account to your crypto wallet quickly. The majority of crypto exchanges also provide a variety of crypto trading tools. Some of the most popular cryptocurrency exchanges for buying, selling, and trading/ investing digital assets include:

• Coinbase

You can buy Bitcoin, Ethereum, Litecoin, Dogecoin, and over 80 other types of cryptocurrencies on Coinbase. This exchange is credible as well as reliable. You can also invest your assets in a lot of ways on the exchange. Coinbase has user-friendly iOS and Android mobile apps. You also have the choice of opening a Coinbase Earn account which will pay you in crypto assets for watching instructional videos.

Coinbase also has two other services: Coinbase Pro for sophisticated traders and Coinbase Prime for institutions and individuals with a net worth of $1 million or more. These services provide several additional benefits, such as the use of safe trading bots, real-time order books, and various other charting tools a user might need to execute trades effectively.

Coinbase isn't the ideal option if you plan to borrow money to trade crypto assets temporarily. It also does not provide the option for futures contracts (these are legal contracts that give you the choice to exchange an asset at a specific price on a forthcoming date).

- Binance.US

Founded in 2019 after the Binance exchange stopped catering its services to US traders, this exchange is largely available to US investors and supports over 50 cryptocurrencies. It, like Coinbase, offers both individual and institutional investors investment possibilities. Its assets are backed by US dollars, and it offers several trading incentives depending on the type of account you choose. Binance.US is also available on iOS and Android devices.

Staking rewards are one notable perk of using this exchange. In particular, holding crypto assets over time may bring you a staking reward from 1% to 10%. For instance, by holding QTUM, a 1%–2% reward could be earned annually.

Other features you can enjoy on this platform include recurring buys (meaning you can place an automatic investment on a predefined schedule), over-the-counter (OTC) trading, and Stablecoins (ones that are backed by US dollars, which can avoid market fluctuations).

A notable downside here is that Binance US is only available to residents of the United States. Furthermore, even in the US, it still has a few geographical restrictions. If you live in Connecticut, Hawaii, Idaho, Louisiana, New York, Texas, or Vermont, for example, you won't be able to access its services. Since its instructional resources are limited, Binance.US may not be the greatest option for new crypto traders.

- Kraken

Just like Coinbase, Kraken offers over 80 cryptocurrencies with a variety of alternatives for all crypto investors. Kraken has a broad worldwide reach. Traders from approximately 200 countries are currently supported by the exchange. It is also a reliable, well-known exchange that is primarily aimed at providing ease of use.

When compared to Coinbase, Kraken also offers futures and margin trading. This means that you can borrow up to five times your account balance to trade crypto assets if you have a margin account. Futures trading is available for Bitcoin, Ethereum, Litecoin, Bitcoin Cash, and Ripple, which allows you to buy or sell an asset at a set price on a specific date. Kraken's iOS and Android mobile app access and educational tools are available to all clients.

The downside here is that currently (2021), US traders can't use Kraken's futures mobile platform. Furthermore, the exchange's counselling and account management services are only available to institutional and high-net-worth clients.

- CEX.IO

CEX.IO is another popular and highly reliable global crypto exchange available today. The platform supports dealers from almost every part of the world, including 48 states in the US. You can buy bitcoin and over 80 other cryptocurrencies from this platform. CEX.IO's instant buy option (only for credit and debit card purchases), mobile app, and crypto-backed loans are available to all customers. For advanced traders, CEX.IO's spot trading function (which allows you to place several sorts of crypto market orders) and margin trading accounts are also available. CEX.IO is available for iOS and Android devices.

This platform has several downsides, though. For one, debit and credit card transactions at CEX.IO tend to be costly. A 2.99 % fee is charged for deposits. Withdrawals made with a Visa card in the United States are subject to a service charge of up to 3% plus an extra $1.20, as well as a commission of up to $3.80. Users of Mastercard might expect a service charge of up to 1.8% plus $1.20. A fee of up to 1.2% + $3.80 is also included.

- Gemini

Gemini is a licensed cryptocurrency exchange that makes purchasing Bitcoin and other altcoins straightforward, quick, and secure. Though Gemini isn't exactly a personal wallet service, its two storage and custody alternatives—Gemini Wallet and Gemini Custody—allow you to store your crypto assets online or in institutional offline storage. In addition, Gemini custody provides cold storage insurance coverage of $200 million. Gemini Earn allows you to earn up to 7.4 % interest on your crypto balance, while Gemini Pay allows you to utilize your assets to make purchases at over 30,000 retail locations across the United States.

For different accounts and account activity, Gemini has several charge schedules. While there is no fee for moving funds via ACH or wire, there is a 3.49% fee for credit or debit card transfers. A limited number of cryptocurrencies are also available on the exchange.

- Bittrex

Bittrex is impossible to beat when it comes to account security. The exchange relies on a multi-stage wallet technique in addition to two-factor authentication to ensure that users' crypto assets are held in secure, cold storage (offline storage). In comparison to other exchanges, Bittrex's transaction fees are significantly lower. Bittrex also has an Instant Buy & Sell tool that allows you to swap bitcoin and other assets instantly. You may use the iOS and Android mobile apps to access this platform, just like the others.

A possible downside here is that this exchange has a maker/taker fee structure depending on your 30-day trading volume (the number of crypto assets you've traded in the previous 30 days). Withdrawals from blockchain/cryptocurrencies incur low network fees. Unlike the other exchanges, though, Bittrex does not charge any fees for deposits (USD deposits and withdrawals have no fees either).

There are several additional trustworthy exchanges, like Robinhood, eToro, Webull, SoFi, and BlockFi. A cryptocurrency exchange is an ideal solution for you if you want a greater range of crypto-specific trading tools and account features.

Forex or CFD Platforms – Any Considerations?

Can we trade cryptocurrencies on a Forex or CFD Platform? A short answer is "Yes". If you want to follow this route, though, there are certain crucial differences between trading crypto on these kinds of platforms and trading on crypto exchanges.

Cryptocurrency Contracts for Difference (also known as CFDs) are traded in most CFD or Forex platforms. By way of a definition, CFD is a type of agreement through which an individual trader can invest in or trade a crypto asset after having entered a contract with the broker, as opposed to opening a position directly on the market.

Here's how it all works: a crypto trader and a CFD/Forex platform enter a contract regarding an underlying asset (Bitcoin for instance). Although these derivatives are still based on actual price fluctuations to determine profits and losses, they do not exchange the actual cryptocurrencies from seller to buyer, like when you perform transactions on crypto exchanges.

This means that you don't have to use any cryptocurrency wallets or keys for making transactions, nor do you care about where to buy cryptocurrencies. CFD trading is preferred by a good number of crypto traders because it significantly reduces the chances of their private data being hacked, making it easier and more convenient for them to focus on the best strategies and techniques to make profits. Without needing to use complex cryptocurrency trading elements, a CFD trader can still make huge profits when the crypto asset price goes favorably with his/her expectations.

Besides the biggest difference, below are some other differences that should be taken to heart.

- The trading rules are dictated by the CFD/Forex platform.

- CFD trading can be leveraged. With leverage trading, a trader can perform trades using borrowed funds from the broker. Typically, such borrowed funds exceed the investors' account balance and hence, this is a great strategy to boost profits by raising one's purchasing power. In the next two chapters, we will discover in detail the pros and cons of using leverage in trading as well as step-by-step guidance in how to operate a trade in one big crypto exchange.

- Unlike the majority of crypto exchanges, on CFD/Forex platforms, you are not limited to cryptocurrency pairs. For instance, you can trade fiat/crypto pairs such as BTC/USD or ETH/USD.

- CFD/Forex platforms only accept fiat currencies for deposits and withdrawals.

Other characteristics you should know before trading on CFD/Forex platforms:

The procedure for CFD trading isn't much different from regular Forex trading. For instance, the available CFDs are normally itemized on the platform along with the tools you might need to start. Again, as is the case with regular forex and stock trading, analyzing the technical and fundamental aspects of the trade coupled with obtaining a balanced trading psyche will help you make good trading choices on the CFD platform.

A detailed understanding of some risk management tools would also help since crypto trading of all forms can be quite volatile. Prices can fluctuate widely sometimes, hence, properly controlling your risk exposure could make a major difference in how much you gain or lose. We'll discuss the various types of analyses you would need for your crypto trading and investing in the next chapter.

News coverage is crucial to the price movements of major cryptocurrency CFDs. Pay attention to the news but do so with great caution. News of regulation changes, hard forks, or cyberattacks can negatively impact the price of an asset. So, remain vigilant but don't forget to do your research. It isn't always easy to predict when market-moving news will be issued but if you keep up with company trends and resources on your assets, you'll rarely be caught unaware.

Finally, watch the price movement on your crypto assets keenly. Sometimes, you can accurately predict the price movement of one crypto asset by observing the price movements of another. For instance, Litecoin was created from Bitcoin's underlying technology. You can think of its assets as Bitcoin clones and they tend to follow Bitcoin's price wherever it goes.

Among the most popular CFD/Forex platforms for trading cryptocurrency are:

- IG: A good platform for beginners with many educational materials.

- Plus500: Famous for its broadest range of cryptocurrencies.

- IC Markets: Best MetaTrader-based platform for trading cryptos.

- AvaTrade: An ideal option for fixed crypto spreads.

Pros and Cons Of Leverage Trading

When it comes to making money with cryptocurrency, leverage trading (or "margin trading") is a common term to most traders. Leverage trading refers to using borrowed capital to raise your buying capacity, which is preferred by traders or speculators, not long-term investors.

If your capital is low, leveraging increases your buying power by allowing you to borrow money from a broker or platform/crypto exchange. Usually, this borrowed capital is much larger than your account balance. You can get access to this borrowed power with just a small amount of money often known as the margin. For example, with only $100 locked as a margin, you can trade up to 10x capital, for example, $5,000, meaning that your trade is leveraged 50 times. Now you trade as if you had $5,000 in your account, and profits and losses are calculated based on such borrowed purchasing capacity.

A new trader should carefully consider the pros and cons of using leveraged trading before moving forward.

Advantages of leverage trading

Minimal investment trading: Traders can take advantage of high leverage to make a huge profit within a short time. Instead of investing a lot of money to buy an "expensive" crypto asset, you can use leverage for trading crypto with as little as a few dozen USD. In the worst case, you would not lose more than your actual account balance. In the best case, your profits would fly.

Profit without interest: Since leverage refers to money borrowed from brokers for trading, traders can make profits without any deductions. Regular trading attracts interest and fees, but for leverage in crypto trading, no interest or fees are paid. Moreover, if the market goes favorably, this technique helps amplify the overall investment of the trader.

Take advantage of market volatility: Crypto trading can be likened to riding on the high seas, no one knows when the waves will come crashing. However, shrewd traders can take advantage of the price fluctuation to use high leverage and make lots of profit. Many investors can use the time to make short investments, allowing them to endure the rough times while still maintaining their profit margin.

Access to exotic pairs: Another significant advantage of leverage trading is that it gives traders access to exotic trading pairs. You can trade two cryptocurrencies paired together (e.g., ETH and BNB). Rather than trading with the currencies themselves, you can speculate on the relative performance of the two.

Disadvantages of leverage trading

Potential huge losses: While discussing the advantages of using leverage in Crypto trading, we are assuming the trade is successful. If a trade goes unsuccessfully, the trader suffers a loss, and the amount of the loss is calculated based on the borrowed capital, which is substantial. In fact, leveraged trading is considered the No.1 reason for traders blowing their trading accounts.

Limited options: Many brokers will not fund your needs if you don't pursue a higher margin. The higher the leverage is, the more dangerous it is for your trading. As a newbie trader, you might want to start with lower leverages (for example: 3x instead of 30x). The lack of safe options may hinder you from achieving small success gradually before opting for more dangerous options.

In short, while leverage trading can offer many opportunities for traders, the relevant risks need to be carefully weighed. In trading with margin, risk or capital management should be put on top priority because your account balance can change drastically if you pay little attention to trading discipline and appropriate management. We will discuss them more later in the book.

Short-Selling: Is It Worth It?

Short-selling or "shorting", as it is commonly called, is a risky but effective way to make money out of falls in the price of an asset. This technique originated outside the context of cryptocurrencies, and it belongs to the realm of derivatives. So before we sink our teeth into crypto shorting per se, it's important we first get a grasp of these underlying concepts, derivatives, and short-selling on their own.

Derivatives are rather infamous financial instruments. For instance, they tend to get blamed for the 2008 financial crisis. Certain types of derivatives specifically linked to mortgages are sometimes seen as the primary cause of financial instruments getting out of control in 2008. Because of their indirect nature, derivatives can be used to push debt more and more, until, at some point, it has nowhere else to go, so it bursts. But this isn't really the fault of derivatives. Instead, it shows how they can be misused, pretty much like any other financial instrument. It's important we don't mix risk with misuse.

Perhaps derivatives are criticized because they are difficult to understand. But it's not that hard to get a general understanding of them. For starters, we should look at their very name: derivative. That means they derive from something else; they themselves aren't the main thing. In mainstream finance, that "something else" could be either another financial instrument or, as I said at the start, an asset. For example, so-called options and futures are all derivatives. They are just contracts specifying the details of an investor's prediction on the behavior of the underlying asset. So you see where the risk comes from, right? If that prediction were wrong, the derivative would result in a loss.

Now let's see what short-selling is about, this time starting with an example. Suppose you're looking at a stock market quote—not from a crypto exchange just yet, but a regular one. You're looking at the price of a commodity, say corn, and you're positive that it will go down in the following days. Why do you know that? Maybe you're a corn specialist, or you've scouted this particular market sector recently. One way or another, you know what you're talking about and have a strong feeling that your prediction is correct. So you borrow stock in a corn company and sell it to other investors who, unlike you, are unaware of the price fall that is about to come. The premise is you intend to sell at a premium, and later, when the price has fallen, you will buy back at the lower price.

If your prediction is correct, shorting will allow you to settle all untied ends in the transaction:

- You'll repay the money owed on the borrowed stock, perhaps with the same money you earned from selling it at a premium.

- You'll acquire cheap stock with the same borrowed funds.

- When prices stabilize, you'll be free to choose whether you wish to keep the stock or sell it again.

By contrast, things seem counterintuitive when a prediction is wrong. In this case, prices would go up, and you might be asking yourself: Why is that a bad thing? Remember, you borrowed this stock at the beginning, so don't actually own it. The only way you can make a profit is if the stock goes down and you're able to sell it for less than you borrowed. That way, you can pay off your debt and keep the remainder to yourself, virtually out of nowhere. But if prices go up instead, and theory has it that there's no limit to how high they can go, then no one will want to buy your borrowed stock because it will be too expensive. You'll end up owing the debt and have an asset you can no longer sell at a profit.

In a nutshell, this is how short-selling works in mainstream finance. On top of that, the common practice among experienced investors is to do it with leverage. In other words, the same procedure, but increasing your position with borrowed money. Our rule of thumb is that shorting with leverage can multiply both your profits and your losses, so it's something you shouldn't do without experience. At the very least, you should watch someone else doing it before you to get some first-hand experience. Let's see how all of this applies in the context of crypto.

Short-selling Crypto 101

The main difference with short-selling traditional assets, as opposed to crypto, comes down to the relation between market price and real price. Since crypto is known to be volatile and highly unpredictable, it is much harder to nail it and know what it will be worth later, even if we're just talking a few hours into the future.

We know the premise of a successful short-selling venture is that we are confident about our prediction on a price, so you see how crypto's notorious unpredictability can quickly become a problem here. In crypto, it is often very hard to set apart the real price from the market price. Most conservative investors will tell you that it just isn't worth trying. However, the reality is that you can make a lot of money this way, provided you do it carefully.

In this case, the asset you borrow through a contract (the derivative in question) is, of course, a cryptocurrency. For example, suppose you were able to predict a Bitcoin recent price fall (since October 2021, it went down from almost $70,000 to just over $50,000). So you may have gone to your exchange of preference back in October and borrowed one bitcoin at its current market price, say $67,000. The next thing you would have had to do is sell it immediately at that price and wait. A couple of months later, after the price falls, you would have had to buy back one bitcoin at the new market price, say $50,000. The difference between these two prices is $17,000, so provided all things worked as described, you would have made quite a profit. First, you would have paid back what you borrowed to the exchange in crypto (one bitcoin), and then you'd get to keep the difference you made in dollars ($17,000).

As you can see, short-selling crypto is different from owning it. This comes from the derivative aspect of it, which was explained earlier. With this technique, you effectively put a sum of fiat currency in the exchange, which is kept as collateral, and this is your contract. You don't ever hold crypto directly because your investment is a short-sell contract, not an actual purchase of the asset.

Short-selling crypto can also be done with leverage, and it's also known as "shorting on margin". Although not all crypto exchanges offer this option, those that do let you choose how much leverage you will use when short-selling a cryptocurrency. This is where you get the 5x, 10x, or 20x, etc., expressions you may have heard. You can go up really high in terms of leverage, but prudent judgment will alert you even at a 5x leverage. Remember our rule of thumb: Leverage increases profits as well as losses. It is not unquestionably wrong to use leverage, but the more you have of it, the riskier a short-selling venture will be. Once again, this is because short-selling is predicated on a price going down, and prices can never fall below zero, but there is no limit to how high they can rise.

Exchanges for Short-selling

Let's address three of the most well-known crypto exchanges: Binance, Kraken, and Coinbase. The options for short-selling you get in each of them aren't the same, so a certain degree of scouting is necessary before choosing the proper venue.

The least complete of the bunch is Coinbase. Unless you get the pro version, short-selling on margin is not available on their platform. Before 2020, any form of on-margin trading wasn't even an option that users had, whether on the pro or the free version. Provided you get the pro version, however, it must be said that Coinbase offers all the options you would get on Kraken or Binance. In either of the three, you can short-sell on margin, trade with futures and CFDs. Another difference to consider is how cumbersome registrations can be. This is a bit of a trade-off because, for instance, Kraken is very quick at this, but then again you also want everything to be legit and safe. In other words, it is often preferable to go through a more thorough registration process and have peace of mind, than to wonder whether you're at any sort of risk because of the exchange itself.

On that note, it's good to know that, as of 2021, FinCEN lists BitYard, BitMart, FTX.US, and CEX.io as their certified exchanges or preference (Palovaara, 2020). Keep in mind that both this latter list and Binance, Kraken, or Coinbase charge a fee in addition to interest on the crypto they loan to you. When doing your calculations as to how much profit short-selling will yield, these sorts of expenses must be factored in.

For the sake of clarity, no matter which exchange you use, placing a short-sell order will work as follows. The crypto will be supplied by the exchange in exchange for a sum you deposit in fiat currency as collateral. From that point on, all trading with the borrowed cryptocurrency of your choice will be done by you, but through their asset. The specifics of your contract will vary depending on the type of your short-sell order and the amount of leverage you choose, if any. Of course, all successful trading will still need to be redeemed at the end by giving back the borrowed crypto to the exchange. Regardless of whether prices go up or down, your debt with the exchange must be repaid.

Some Certified Short-selling Methods

We have already reviewed the process by which an investor can short-sell crypto, but there are a number of variants on top of that. Here I explain what they are about, what you get from them, and what sorts of risks they entail.

Futures

A futures contract requires you to specify both the time and price at which an asset, in this case crypto, will be bought or sold. The difference here is that your bet is actually placed on the price going up. If this doesn't happen, you can always resell the futures contract, albeit certainly at a loss. This implies that both rising and lowering prices offer an opportunity for investors. In a bullish market, you can buy futures contracts. Whereas in a bearish market, you have the option of short-selling.

In traditional finance, this technique is usually used to better forecast your finances. For example, a pizza restaurant and a wheat farmer can lock in on a futures contract that will benefit both parties. On one side of this deal, the pizza restaurant can plan ahead knowing that the price of wheat won't vary, whereas on the other side the farmer can prevent losses in case wheat's market price goes down. Now, in the context of crypto, the two parties involved are the exchange and yourself. You don't forecast for your business, but rather hitch to an uphill trend in prices as you see it coming.

Crypto exchanges settle these contracts on a daily basis, so your balance will be updated constantly and move up or down depending on how the day went. What you need to keep in mind is that the price set in the futures contract may differ from the market price if your prediction is wrong. In cases like this, you can trade the contract before the maturity date and hop off the wagon. But this of course will cost an extra fee for early removal.

CFDs

As I said a little earlier, CFD stands for Contract For Difference. This method is aimed at simplifying the hassle of borrowing crypto, in case it wasn't plain enough for you or you wished to have an extra gig on the side. With this instrument, you don't borrow, sell, and then pay back. Instead, you just buy the CFD contract stating that the price of a specific cryptocurrency will go down. Thereafter you just need to wait and get paid the difference when prices go down. Of course, you're the one who pays the difference in case your prediction was wrong.

An investor has the option to either buy or sell a CFD depending on where they think prices will go. As a general rule, you're supposed to buy these contracts when you think prices will go up and sell them when you think they will go down.

Your position, like that of all other short-selling instruments, can be leveraged to increase the chances for profit. Since this is a risky move, there is a way to shield against extremely bad outcomes, and these are called limits. Setting a limit means you automatically specify a price limit at which the CFD will be traded, so you can bail before things get too bad.

Options

These are similar to futures in almost every respect. An investor buys options to reserve the right to either buy or sell an asset at a pre-set price, regardless of what the actual market price ends up being. That much is the same in futures contracts as in options, except options give you the ability to choose whether or not you wish to exercise that contract, hence the name. When the maturity date arrives and you deem it unprofitable to use the option, you can withhold the contract. Options also come in two types: one to call and one to put a transaction. The call option means you agree to buy and the put option means you agree to sell.

A good thing about options is that even if your prediction fails, you only need to pay for the contract. There is a limit to what you can lose, by contrast to plain short-selling or futures. Now, in case you didn't have enough jargon already, there are two other terms to learn here. One is the strike price and the other is the spot price. The former refers to the agreed-upon price and the latter refers to the current market price. Naturally, these two may differ and this is actually how option buyers and sellers stand to make a profit. Put simply, a buyer will want the strike price to be lower than the spot price so they can settle the option and trade the asset at a premium. And vice versa, the seller will want the strike price to be higher so they can earn a difference from the current spot price.

Step-By-Step Guidance On Trade Operation

To better assist you with a visual illustration of how to enter and exit trades in real life, I will present below the step-by-step guidance on placing your trade on Binance.US – one of the most common crypto exchanges with low fees and a user-friendly interface. This exchange provides the options of using leverage, and you can optimize your trade efficiency as stated below. Although the trade execution process may not be exactly the same on other platforms, the principle will not be much different.

First, let's discover a very important and interesting part of placing a trade order: understanding different types of trade orders.

Market orders

Market orders are the simplest trade orders where you place a command to buy/sell the cryptocurrency at the currently available price. By clicking on the buy/sell button, the order will be implemented nearly immediately. A market long order will match the closest ask price (what sellers are willing to sell for) and a market short order will match the closest bid price (what buyers are willing to buy for).

Traders often choose this order type when they want their trades to be executed immediately, either to avoid missing good trade opportunities in the market or to cut losses. Cryptocurrencies that are well-established and have considerable trading volume are more appropriate for market orders.

Limit orders

Unlike a market order, a limit order allows you to buy the crypto at a specific price (a better one) instead of the current price. A buy limit order allows you to buy at a lower price while a sell limit order allows you to sell at a higher price. With that said, the limit order may not be implemented, depending on whether the price reaches your desired level or not. Limit orders ensure that you won't pay higher in case of a long order and won't sell lower in case of a short order.

Limit orders are preferred when you identify the current price is still not the ideal one for trade execution, and you are not in a rush for entering a trade. For example, you determine that there is a better chance of Bitcoin reversing upward when it comes to the $50,000 level from the current price of $55,000, and put a buy limit order at $50,000. If you think Bitcoin will reverse downward when it reaches the $70,000 mark, then a sell limit (or take-profit order) will be placed at the $70,000 level.

Stop-limit orders

In many online crypto exchanges, you may see this type of order.

A stop-limit order has two elements: a stop price and a limit price. When the stop price is reached, the limit price will be triggered.

For example, suppose the last traded price of ETH is $3,950, and you see that there is resistance around $4,000. If you think the price will go higher after reaching the $4,000 mark, you can put a stop-limit order to buy more ETH at $4,050, for example, after it reached the $4,000 level. In this example, the $4,000 is the stop price, and the $4,050 is the limit price (or the trigger price).

The stop price and limit price can be the same. Yet, it is advisable to set your limit price slightly higher than the stop price in case of a buy order and a little bit lower than the stop price in a sell order.

Similar to a limit order, a stop-limit order is suitable for a trader who doesn't want to spend her time watching market movements so closely.

OCO orders

A "One Cancels the Other" ("OCO") order includes two different orders that are placed at the same time, but only one of them is executed. When one order is fully or partially executed, the other is automatically deleted.

OCO is considered the combination of a limit order and a stop-limit order, providing versatility for traders to participate in the market.

For example: Let's say Bitcoin is moving in a range between the support level of $50,000 and the resistance level of $60,000. You want to trade in the direction of a potential breakout, but have no bias about the future movement of the market. In this case, you can opt for an OCO order to either buy on resistance breakout (above $60,000) or sell if the price drops below the $50,000 support level.

If used appropriately, an OCO order is a perfect option in helping you securely execute and manage your trades, either by locking some handsome profits or reducing risks. We will have some specific examples to illustrate this idea soon.

Now that we've learned about four types of trade orders, let's look at how you can enter and exit trades in the Binance.US exchange. We will explore both spot trading and margin trading (or leverage trading).

In the next section below, we'll go step-by-step through how to enter and exit a trade on Binance.US. Please do not worry about the candlestick colors. Instead, focus on the price movement only so that you can understand the meaning of the trade option. In the next chapters of the book, we'll use much more detailed chart illustrations.

Spot trading on Binance.US

Spot trading means "exchanging one crypto for another". In spot trading, you won't use leverage, meaning that you just process the trade transaction based on the money you have.

First, visit the Binance.US website and log in with your account information. Using a two-step verification code will maximize your account safety.

Second, click on any cryptocurrency appearing on the home page to go directly to the spot trading interface. A larger list of cryptocurrencies can be found by clicking at the "View more markets" at the bottom of the list.

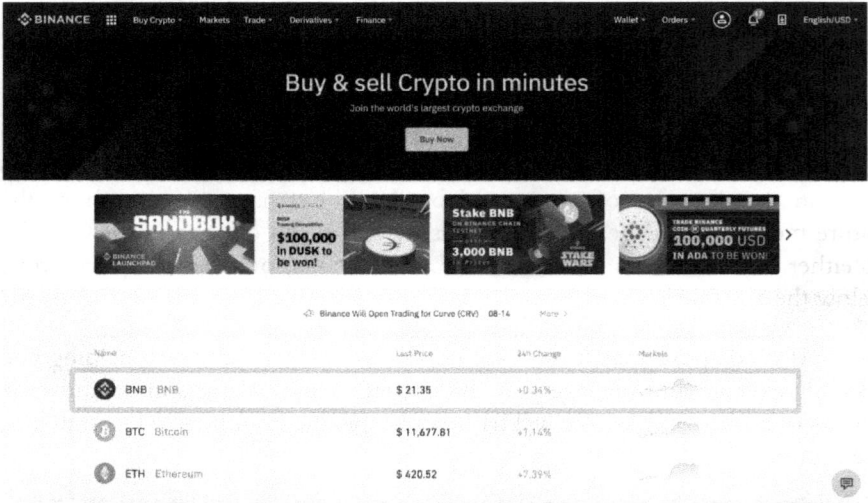

Source: Binance.US

At this point, you will be at the spot trading screen. Here is a summary of what will be available in the interface.

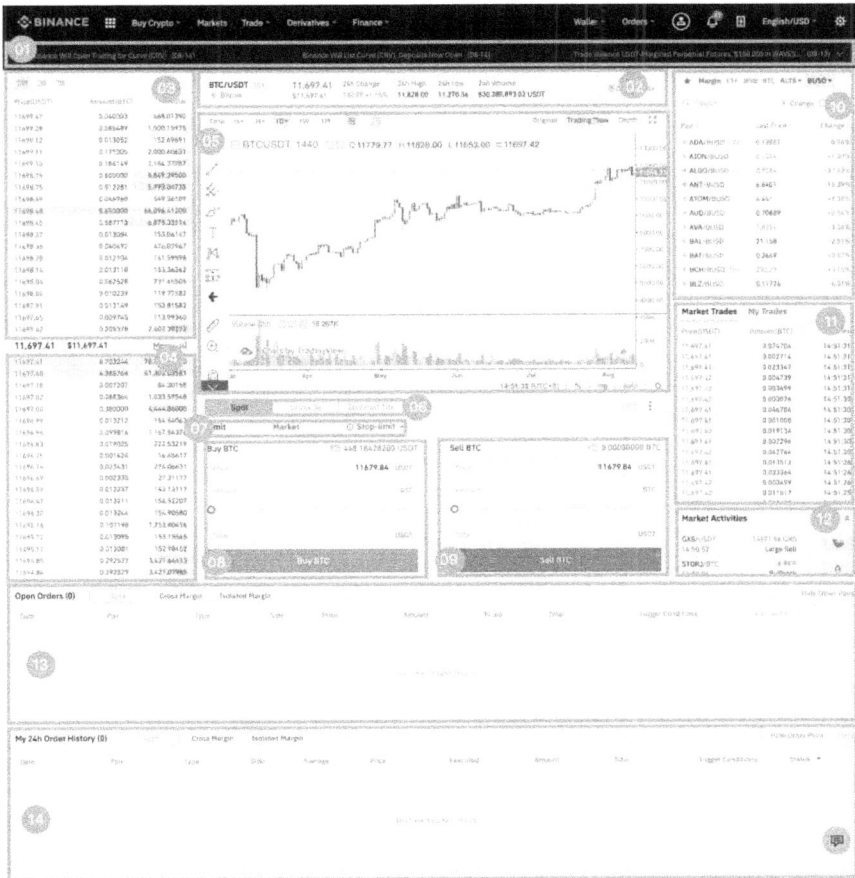

Source: Binance.US

On the left-hand side, you can see the order book section, including the asking price on the top (3) and the bid price on the bottom (4). Located in the top right corner is the market list containing the supported trading pairs in each market (10). The middle section shows the real-time market candlestick chart and the available technical indicators (5).

The main trading section is located below the candlestick charts, with the buying area on the left and the selling area on the right ((8) and (9)). Before deciding which crypto to buy or sell, as well as the trading volume, you should determine which type of orders will you take (i.e limit, market, or stop-limit order).

Below the order section, you can monitor your trade by looking at the order history section (14).

• Buy crypto

Before making transactions, you need to have crypto in your spot account. You can either buy crypto via different methods or, if you already have crypto in other wallets, you can deposit your crypto to your spot account.

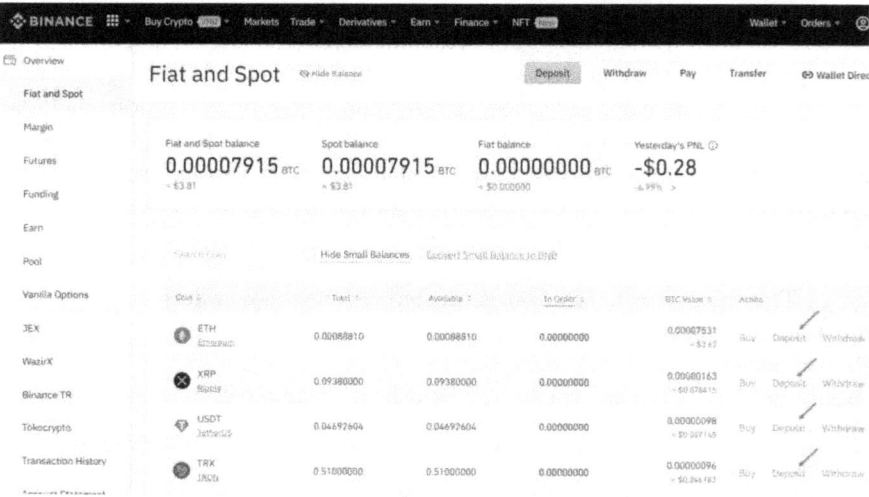

Let's say you opt for a buy limit order for Bitcoin (BTC) at 10,000 USDT (or Tether USD - a stablecoin which is approximately $10,000), insert the price at which you want to buy BTC, and the amount of BTC you would want to buy. Click the buy button, and done!

Source: Binance.US

Once the market price reaches ten 10,000 USDT, your order will be completed, and you can track it in the trade history section, and you can also see the purchased amount in your spot wallet.

If the price of BTC does not reach 10,000 USDT and you no longer want to wait on the order, you can click "cancel" in the open orders section to cancel the order.

Now, you may wonder what the "cross 3x" and "isolated 10x" means. Don't worry, we will learn about them very soon.

• Sell crypto

If you want to sell BTC at a market price, you can use a market order. In the sell panel, the price has been marked "market" for you. And you just need to enter the amount of BTC you want to sell. Click "sell BTC", and done! You can visit your spot wallet to recheck your updated amount of USDT.

Source: Binance.US

Leverage trading on Binance.US

As I stated above, using leverage in trading gives you more power to multiply your trading profits. In the section below, we will learn how to maximize your trading power up to 10x time to make the best of the market movements on Binance.US.

• How to buy using leverage

Let's assume the bitcoin price is currently at 10,000 USDT. You expect it to rise and you want to purchase some bitcoin.

We've seen that a spot transaction is for exchanging purposes, meaning no leverage is used. You can see there are two options next to the "spot" button: Cross 3x and Isolated 10x. These options give you the chance to increase your trading power to 3x and 10x respectively.

Source: Binance.US

Let's assume we use isolated margin and trade with a limit order.

Step 1: Transfer 10,000 BUSD (another stablecoin, equivalent to $10,000) as collateral from your spot account to your BTC/BUSD margin account.

Step 2: In the buy panel, click on "borrow", input 10,000 at the price level. Then, fill in the BTC amount you want to buy, and click "margin buy BTC".

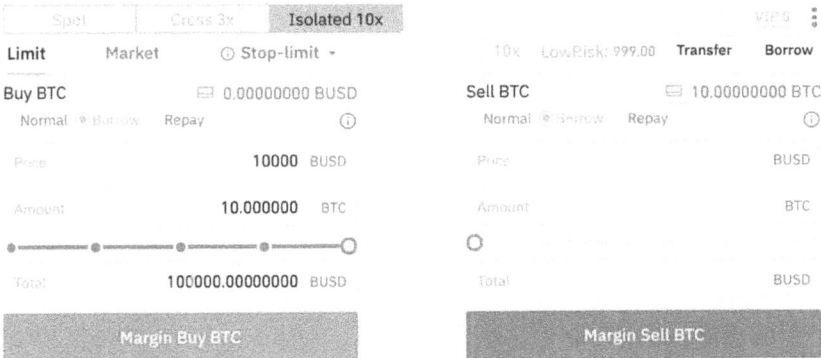

Source: Binance.US

Once the order is completed, you would have borrowed 90,000 BUSD and bought 10 BTC at the price of 10,000 BUSD.

After some time, let's say the price goes up to 11,000 BUSD, and you want to take profit. To do this, you will use the repay function and sell 10 BTC at 11,000 BUSD each.

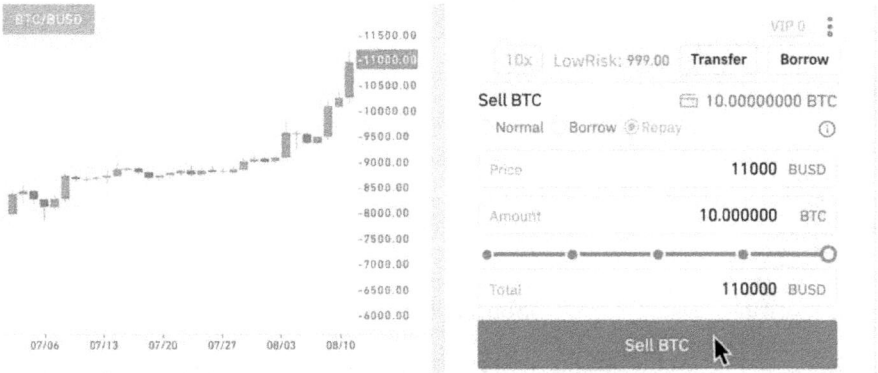

Source: Binance.US

Then, the initially borrowed 90,000 BUSD will be refunded automatically. If the handling fees and interest are ignored, you will have 20,000 BUSD in your isolated margin account and earn 10,000 BUSD, equivalent to 100% profit.

The market may go opposite to your expectation, which is why you should use a stop-loss for your order. As I mentioned below, OCO is a great choice for setting take-profit and stop-loss level with one action (setting a double-order).

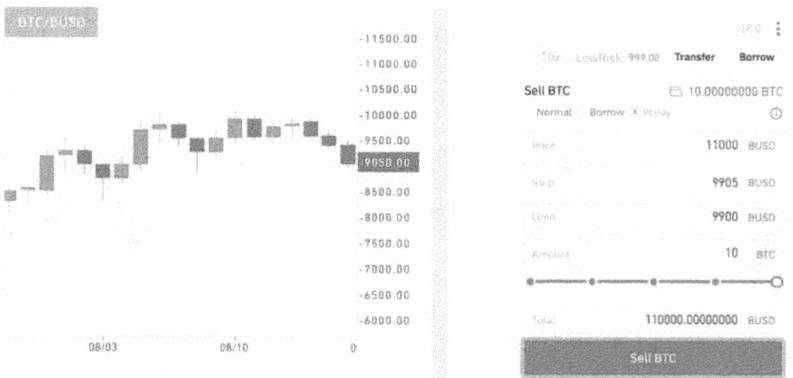

Source: Binance.US

Looking at the image above, in the sell section, select "repay", then input the take-profit price in the "price" line.

The next two lines ("stop" and "limit") are the two components in the stop-limit order we mentioned above. In this case, let's say you choose 9,905 and 9,900 as stop price and limit price respectively. Next, you input the amount of Bitcoin you want to buy before clicking the "Sell BTC" button.

Now, we have an OCO order which consists of one limit order and one stop-limit order. Yet, only one of them can be executed. If the price falls down to the 9,905 level, a sell order will be triggered at the 9,900 level, and the limit order will be canceled. Whereas, if the price increases to 11,000 level first, the limit order is initiated and the stop-limit order will be cancelled.

- How to sell using leverage

Still on the previous example where the Bitcoin price is at 10,000 BUSD, perhaps you think the price will drop in the future. You would process the similar steps as in the long position, but in the opposite direction.

Let's assume we use the cross 3x leverage and a limit order.

Step 1: Transfer 10,000 BUSD as collateral from your spot account to your margin account. On the BTC/BUSD trading page.

Step 2: In the buy panel, click on "borrow", input 10,000 at the price level. Then, fill in the BTC amount you want to sell, and click "Margin sell BTC".

Source: Binance.US

Once the order is completed, you would have borrowed 2 BTC and sold them at the price of 10,000 BUSD each.

Let's assume that after some time, the BTC price falls to 7,000 BUSD. Then, you will use the repay function, and buy 2 BTC at 7,000 BUSD each.

Source: Binance.US

Then, the initially borrowed 2 BTC (equivalent to 14,000 BUSD) will be refunded automatically. If the handling fees and interest are ignored, you would have 16,000 BUSD in your margin account. Compared to the initially deposited 10,000 BUSD, you have 6,000 BUSD in profit – equivalent to 60%.

Again, the market may go in an opposite direction, and an OCO order could still be used both for stop-loss and take-profit functions.

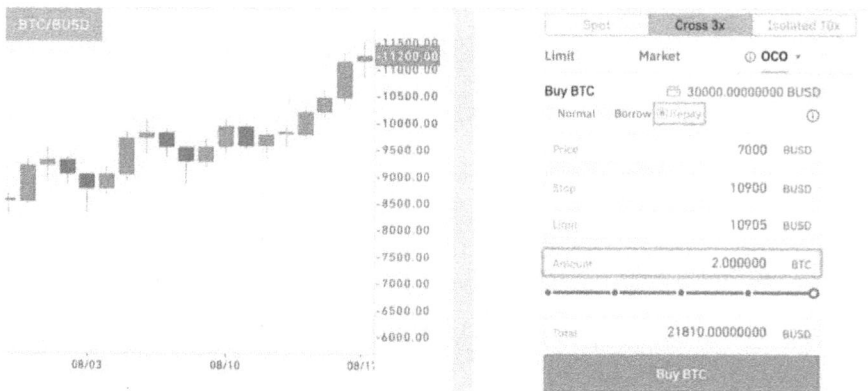

Source: Binance.US

We process the repay function as shown in the picture above. In the buy section, select "repay", input the take-profit, the stop, and the limit price. Let's assume they are 7,000; 10,900; and 10,905 respectively. The stop and the limit price together form the stop-limit order (or the stop-loss). Next, enter the amount of BTC you want to take profit/set stop-loss before hitting the "Buy BTC" button.

Now, we have an OCO order which consists of one limit order and one stop-limit order. If the price rises to the 10,900 level, a buy order will be triggered at 10,905, and the limit order at 7,000 level will be canceled. Whereas, if the price falls to the 7,000 level first, a buy trade would be triggered here and the stop-limit order would be canceled.

Chapter 3: Choosing Cryptos

The Need To Pick A Great Crypto.

There is a wide variety of trading and investing strategies that we can utilize to make the best use of price movements. Profiting in any financial market all boils down to buying low and selling high, or selling and then buying back at a lower price. Yet, determining the highs and lows in trading/investing could become extremely difficult if traders don't pay enough attention to market analysis.

It's important to note that mere market analyses cannot ensure any trade or investment success. Its primary and sole function is to equip traders with necessary information on the crypto assets they trade/invest in.

There are some popular methods of market analysis crypto traders and investors often use in their decision-making process to work out the best entry and exit points in the financial market. In the next sections below, we will explore three types of market analysis that could put you in a better position to make a winning trading/investing decision.

Fundamental Analysis: Core Values Really Matter

Fundamental analysis is a means of assessing an asset's true value. Certain information that underlies crypto assets is studied to determine if the asset is undervalued or overvalued. While fundamental analysis alone may not help traders to make a trading decision, it helps to form a good opinion on the asset's value. In other words, via fundamental analysis, we have a better idea of whether a crypto asset is worth trading/investing.

Factors To Consider Under Fundamental Analysis of Crypto Assets

With this approach, the primary purpose is to lower your investment risk by assessing the potentials of crypto asset's return before committing your funds. There are three main metrics you can use to conduct your research with this approach:

1. The blockchain or on-chain metrics

For your research, the blockchain network is a great resource. The top cryptocurrency exchanges have now developed various forms and reporting tools to provide investors related useful data they need (such as the number of active users, the total number of daily transactions, transaction value) to make better trading or investment choices. Some major metrics to look for when researching a blockchain include:

- The hash rate of the blockchain

The hash rate refers to the total computing power required in mining to execute cryptographic calculations on a Proof-of-Work (PoW) blockchain. Without getting too technical, the way it works is that the higher the hash rate, the more miners will be motivated to mine for profit, and the network will be more secure. Conversely, miners may find the coin unprofitable if the hash rate continues to fall. Lower hash rates may suggest that investors are losing interest.

- The number of active blockchain addresses

The number of active blockchain addresses is another good metric for you to conduct a fundamental analysis of an asset. One of the most straightforward methods to tackle this is by tallying up the number of transmitting and receiving addresses over time. To evaluate activity and interest in a coin or token, you can also sum up the active addresses transacting with that coin over days, weeks, or months and analyze their fluctuation. This serves to give you more information on the real value of the blockchain you intend to invest in.

- Fees and transaction value

The fees represent the demand on the blockchain network, and the number of transactions competing to be added to the blockchains. Each cryptocurrency can have its transaction fees, which will inevitably rise over time. The amount of fees paid over time provides you with a notion of how safe the coin or token is.

Also, the fundamental analysis takes the assessment of transaction value into account. On the whole, a consistently high transaction value indicates the crypto is in good circulation.

Best platforms for analyzing on-chain data: santiment.net, cryptoquant.com, messari.io, glassnode.com, dune.xyz, nansen.ai, intotheblock.com, breadcrumbs.app

2. The financial metrics

This approach aims to generate a quantifiable value that an investor can use to assess an asset's prospects. It entails a firm grasp of the asset's trading conditions, such as liquidity, market reaction, and other related factors. To do this effectively, take the following into account:

• Market capitalization or market cap

The market capitalization value represents the total worth of all the coins created on a network. It's computed by multiplying the current market price of a single coin by the total number of coins in circulation. While it's hard to determine exactly how many coins are in circulation due to forgotten currencies, lost wallets, and irrecoverable keys, market capitalization provides a rough estimate of a coin's network value.

• Liquidity & Trading Volume

The ease with which an asset can be bought and sold is referred to as its liquidity. An asset's liquidity is strong if it can be bought or sold fast without any significant alterations to its market value. Another sign of a coin's ability to maintain momentum is its trading volume. This refers to how many units of the asset have changed hands over a specific time period. You are likely to retain your profits on a crypto asset if an upward trend in value is accompanied by a high trading volume.

• Supply circulation

The entire number of coins accessible to the public is referred to as the circulating supply of a cryptocurrency. Because coins can be burned, this figure is constantly updated over time. In a centralized supply, developers can raise the number of coins or tokens in circulation. For example, mining activities can increase the circulating supply of a mineable cryptocurrency.

Best sites for an insight of cryptos' financial metrics: coinmarketcap.com, coinlobster.com, glassnode.com, messari.io, CoinGecko, tradingview.com.

3. The project metrics

"Project metrics" uses a qualitative way to assess a cryptocurrency's performance. This approach concentrates on both internal and external variables, such as the cryptocurrency's purpose and how it runs. Most of these data are available on the cryptocurrency project's website. Here are some elements to keep in mind concerning the project metrics.

- Background information

A list of the team members who developed the crypto-asset should be available on its site. Researching team biographies and their track records will provide you with more insight into the project's likelihood of success. Look at the team's past accomplishments and experience. You should also consider the position of any early backers or supporters of the asset to gain more information on its legitimacy.

- The white paper

This is a technical document that describes the project's goals and operations. It should include details on Blockchain technology solutions, currency use cases, scheduled features and upgrades, token economics and sale details, and ultimately, information about the founders. Examine the white paper closely and keep an eye out for third-party reviews about the cryptocurrency and its project.

- Competitive analysis

Don't forget to research the asset's competition. The landscape in which each project must compete is identified by doing thorough research for market rivals. Understanding a broader ecology is critical for you to accurately assess the asset's potential.

- The asset's roadmap

Most crypto products have a roadmap for the future that shows a schedule for test nets, releases, and new features to come. The road map should provide a good potential for future developments. Use this reference guide to confirm whether or not the roadmap can help you fulfill your investment goals.

- Tokenomics and Utility

The value and price of cryptocurrencies are determined by supply and demand. The higher the price, the higher the demand is in comparison to supply. The role that a token can play is represented by its utility or usefulness. More users and attention may be attracted to a token with more real-world use cases.

In short, fundamental analysis will equip you with a comprehensive picture of a company. As liquid exchange platforms, crypto trading bots, and active forums all contribute to a thriving ecosystem, the resources available for this type of analysis are also expanding. In cryptocurrency markets, investors who conduct thorough research and perform fundamental analysis stand a better chance to benefit handsomely.

Sentiment Analysis: The Smell of The Market

Market sentiment refers to investors' general emotional reactions to an asset. In essence, crypto market sentiment analysis is a psychological assessment of the elements that drive cryptocurrency price movement. This is important because the way investors feel about a cryptocurrency can have a significant impact on its market cycles and price. It can have significant effects if enough traders act on these ideas, thoughts, and feelings. For instance, Elon Musk's tweets have had a significant impact on the price of Bitcoin (a bullish sentiment).

Rates of funding

A cryptocurrency's funding rate is a trackable parameter that often correlates with market sentiment. Funding rates are the payments made to traders on a regular basis based on the price differentials between cryptocurrency everlasting contracts and the currency or token's spot prices.

When the rates are positive, the market is usually optimistic, and long traders will compensate short traders. Negative funding, on the other hand, indicates that in a downtrend market, short traders will be paying long traders. Coinlend, CryptoLend, DeFi Rate, and LoanScan are some of the tools available to track funding rates.

Sentiment indices

How can you tell the opinion of the market on crypto assets? The asset's volatility, market momentum, investor replies to surveys, Google Trends, junk bond demand, and other factors can all come in handy here. If the market is uncertain or downright afraid to invest in an asset you have researched into and found to be sound, it might be wise for you to buy such assets. Conversely, a greedy market is a good time to sell.

- Social media analysis

When gauging the crypto market mood, keep an eye on Twitter, Discord Channels, Telegram, and Reddit. A social community that is active and engaged will have a large number of followers and meaningful social engagement across platforms. Google Trends is another popular way to evaluate Bitcoin market interest. Google Trends displays search activity for a certain keyword phrase, allowing you to see whether Bitcoin searches are heading upward or downward. A hype attracts more market participants, implying that a positive feeling is on the way.

- Monitor the whales

A cryptocurrency whale is an investor who accumulates significant amounts of cryptocurrency and conducts large-scale transactions across many blockchains. Whale watching is the practice of keeping an eye on major cryptocurrency players. Whale watchers find the trades of large market participants and then mirror those trades. Crypto whales are often experts with specific knowledge. Some popular resources for following their trade activities are ClankApp, Whale Alert (Twitter), WhaleTrace.

While mirroring the whales can be beneficial sometimes, it may also result in stress and losses if not carefully assessed. In Chapter 10, we'll go deeper into it with a typical example among new traders.

Market Sentiment Analysis Indicators

Market sentiment analysis is a critical component of effectively predicting a crypto asset's worth or value. If the prices are on the rise, then the market sentiment on the asset in question is deemed bullish. Conversely, if the prices are on a decline, then the market sentiment is deemed to be bearish.

The following are some of the most important indicators you should adopt for the purposes of your market sentiment analysis study:

- Fear & Greed Index.

This is a measure of how fearful and greedy people are concerning a crypto asset. The Fear & Greed Index is a global market mood indicator used in traditional stock markets. The sentiment index has a numerical value between 0 and 100, with 0 representing extreme fear and 100 representing excessive greed. The Bitcoin Fear & Greed Index is a good example of this. It measures how worried or greedy people are about cryptocurrencies in cryptocurrency marketplaces by considering several variables. On the whole, the higher the index is, the more dangerous it is to open or remain in your position in the crypto market.

- The Bull & Bear Index

The Bull & Bear Index (BBI) is another popular and trustworthy Bitcoin mood gauge that focuses on social media indicators. The BBI gathers about 93 attitudes by utilizing artificial intelligence to analyze themes and conversations from the Bitcoin Forum, Reddit, Twitter, and the market movement of digital assets. An extremely bearish market is represented by a value of zero, whereas an extremely bullish market is represented by a value of one.

- DeFi Total Value Locked

DeFi's total value locked (TVL) is a reliable indicator of the company's and markets' health. The entire current supply, the maximum supply, and the current cryptocurrency value are all taken into account by TVL. The TVL ratio is used by traders to determine if an asset is overvalued or undervalued. Its value is calculated by multiplying the current supply of an asset in circulation by its current trade price, then divided by the market capitalization. When the TVL ratio falls below 1, it usually means a DeFi asset is undervalued, and vice versa.

- Altcoin gainers and losers

Altcoin gainers and losers are the top-performing or collapsing coins across various time periods, similar to a continually shifting scoreboard. Rather than manually charting gains and losses across several cryptocurrencies, investors can utilize one of the many cryptocurrency investment trackers available. CoinMarketCap, CoinCodex, and CoinGecko are a few examples.

Cryptocurrency sentiment analysis is an important instrument to have in your crypto toolbox. However, just like the fundamental analysis, this type of analysis should not be used individually. When used in combination with other types of market analysis, we will have a much better picture of the crypto price and its potentials.

In addition to the above points, the fundamental analysis and technical analysis themselves can also be included in measuring sentiment analysis. In the next section, we'll learn about the most important type of analysis that occupies nearly half of this book – the technical analysis.

Technical Analysis: Honing Your Skills and Techniques

Technical analysis refers to a method of predicting any future movements in an asset's price levels by examining its previous price histories and movement. It focuses on identifying better trading and investment opportunities by analyzing historical trading actions and chart patterns.

Technical analysis focuses purely on price action and trend analysis. The best thing about this approach is that you don't need an economics degree to adopt it. Anyone who understands the basic tenets of supply and demand and is willing to study a few other market factors can grasp this quickly and start realizing more profits from trades.

How does it work?

In technical analysis, traders and investors will use past price behaviors to anticipate what may happen in the future. The key idea here is that asset prices do not fluctuate at random. On the contrary, price movements have certain general rules and characteristics, and if you adopt the technical approach to your crypto research, you can master how to read an asset's price history like you would read a map to forecast what will happen next.

The major task undertaken by technical analysts is to analyze the broader market fluctuations to determine the precise point from where an asset's price has the best chance of moving. This approach necessitates using some tools, but you can master these with practice. We will dig deeper into these tools and how to use them the most effectively in the next part of this book. Yet, let's first discuss some of the basic tools in the crypto market:

• Price action

Price action is a trading method preferred by a lot of traders due to its simplicity and effectiveness. This method makes use of price fluctuations and volume data to help traders predict what may happen next, regardless of which assets they are trading. This process is typically applied in connection with candlestick charts, which are used in the assessment of market trends. Crypto volatility is not as easy to predict as any investor would wish or expect, but there is historical data for reference, which you can use for this purpose.

• Candlestick

Candlesticks are among the most commonly used tools in technical analysis of the crypto market, and Japanese candlesticks are favored by most traders. The basic principle in using candlesticks is to rely on the past and present candle formation indicated in the chart to predict what may happen next. Price reversal and continuation setups are commonly seen in candlestick charts. The picture below shows some example of reversal patterns, signaling the reversal of the trend:

We will cover all trading techniques in connection with candlesticks later in this book, so don't worry. This just gives you an idea of what candlesticks pattern trading is about.

• Momentum and trend

Market momentum and the underlying trend influence an asset's price action. When there is vigorous purchasing or selling pressure, an asset's price can rise dramatically or drop abruptly. Conversely, when the trends are corrective, the market takes a rest, and the price fails to make a new high (in an uptrend) or a new low (in a downtrend). To see how both of these trends work, take a look at the following graphic example:

The price of Bitcoin swung swiftly in May 2021, going from $60,000 to $30,000 in less than two weeks. The image above shows this aggressive move in Bitcoin's price. Buying and keeping a cryptocurrency is advantageous once the trend is identified correctly. In trading, the trend is your friend until it bends.

Technical Analysis Indicators

There was no computerized charting system in the early days of technical analysis. Traders used to record prices using a pen and paper. Trading has become more efficient as a result of technological advancements, particularly in the cryptocurrency industry. Traders can utilize technical indicators to predict market movement better.

Technical indicators display the current price position based on a set of criteria. As a trader, you should be familiar with some key indicators to get a trustworthy result from technical analysis. Each of these indicators will be discussed in depth in later chapters, with specific examples and tips on how to use them.

- The Relative Strength Index (RSI)

The Relative Strength Index (RSI) is a momentum indicator that depicts data on a scale of 1–100. It displays an asset's overbought and oversold areas under various circumstances. When the RSI indicator falls below 30, it suggests that the price is under bearish pressure. When the RSI indicator rises above 70, it indicates that an asset is overbought and may undergo price fluctuations. RSI signals, like most other technical indicators, are more efficient and reliable when used in conjunction with long-term trends and other indicators.

- Moving Averages (MA)

For any given timeframe, a moving average displays the average price of a crypto trading asset over time. For example, the average price of the previous 20 days' price changes is represented by the MA20 line. The use of the MAs is based on the idea of anticipating price movement via past price behaviors. Crossovers and divergences from the historical average lines can be used to identify bullish and bearish signals.

- Fibonacci tools

Fibonacci trading tools come from the infinite mathematical sequence introduced by the Italian mathematician Leonardo Pisano Bogollo in the 13th century. The two most famous Fibonacci techniques are retracements and extensions, which are widely used by nearly every trader in identifying support and resistance levels.

Fibonacci is treated as a leading indicator because it can identify potential key levels in the future instead of providing delayed feedback to traders as many other technical indicators do. Fibonacci works best in the financial market when combined with other market tools and techniques. In Chapter 9, we will explore in detail one of the Fibonacci tools preferred by most professional traders.

In summary, a good trading choice should be a combination of all three types of market analysis. Since crypto assets tend to follow their historical price actions, technical analysis is considered the most popular and important type of analysis in trading or investing crypto. Even if applying technical analysis does not guarantee 100% correct signals, it will assist you in comprehending the rationale behind each crypto price movement. Once you have a firm grasp on this, you can optimize your investments to generate more consistent returns.

PART TWO

INTO THE BATTLE

IN THIS PART

- Discover my trading philosophies that will hugely differentiate you from other traders/investors out there.

- Explore three fantastic trading ingredients that no one will ever tell you in the crypto context.

- Step-by-step guide to the four most powerful strategies in crypto trading/investing.

- Discover the art of using Dollar Cost Averaging (DCA), Average True Range (ATR), and Moving Average (MA) in optimizing your trading results.

Chapter 4: My Trading Philosophies

The crypto market notoriously displays drastic changes in price within short periods of time. It is considered the most volatile asset in the financial market. Such volatility can cause confusion and emotional chaos within each trader, which is the number one reason trading accounts can be destroyed.

Many consider crypto trading to be a risky (but potentially very profitable) venture. Luckily, there are always secrets or protections to help prevent things from becoming worse and to keep traders on track for consistent profits

In this chapter, we will discuss the two most important philosophies that each trader should understand and respect in every circumstance to keep them on track. Failure to do so could put traders in BIG trouble when the prices go against their expectations.

It is all about probability in trading

While most of us emphasize the need for obtaining a good risk-reward ratio in each trade (which I will cover in one important chapter at the end of the book), it should be combined with a deep understanding of the probability in trading so that your expectations are aligned appropriately. In trading, expectations affect everything.

According to scientists, our minds are wired to play a mindful game in connection with the success probability of a trade. Once a trade is initiated, we tend to be more confident than we should be, ignoring the likelihood of the inevitable dangers in this endeavor and believing in a better probability of winning than what exists in reality.

This way of thinking is also called confirmation bias, where we strive to seek reasons to prove that we're right.

The Law Of Probability In Trading

In trading, the probability of a winning trade is roughly between 40-60 percent, depending on market conditions. It means that at any point in time, we SHOULD and MUST ASSUME that we only have around 40-60 percent chance of winning, and the possibility of losing is around 40-60 percent, too. I use the word "around" because it may be higher or lower in a particular circumstance, but it is NEVER 100%. Simple as that.

The question is: Can we expect a long-term sustainable winning if we lose around half of our trades?

The answer is: Yes and No.

You can be successful with just 40% of the total trades (or even less) and still be profitable as long as you manage the trades (including managing your own emotions) correctly. Conversely, you can have a much higher rate of successful trades and still lose money overall (or even blow your trading account) due to poor trade management. Because of that, we have to manage our trades appropriately in both winning and losing circumstances.

When you do something in your own life and fail 50% of the time, you may feel depressed which can lead to subsequent disastrous outcomes. We hate being wrong and love being right. Hence, losing 50% of your total trades may be considered a failure as long as we consider winning trades as "right" and losing trades as "wrong". Worse, our brain absorbs such information and tells us that if we continue to trade that way, we will fail. As a result, we strive to increase the winning rates, only to bring about more and more losing ones and eventually quit the mission.

On the other hand, a seasoned trader is confident that a 40-60 percent winning rate is more than enough to make consistent profits if he focuses on clear market signals according to his set of trading rules, coupled with careful risk management

Be Profitable Or Be Right

But we all want to be right. You may doubt your ability to rearrange your belief after only a few words of advice from one (profitable) trader.

It is best to be both profitable and right, isn't it?

Yes, you can be right 100 percent of the time and be profitable, too, if you think of "being right" as following exactly the rules set in your trading system. The system will take care of everything for a trade to be executed, including the profitability and the risk/reward ratio.

The system should take care of our beliefs, too. It does not matter what is present on the trading chart. If something happens that meets all criteria in the system, then it is time to take a trade. Otherwise, just remain on the sidelines. If you follow your system 100% for a long enough period without generating consistent profits, it may be time to make necessary changes to your system or switch to another one.

As long as you follow your system, you should and must accept that it can be a losing one. As I said above, you will be right 40-60 percent of the time. There is NO rule in the financial market, and there is NO rule in how candlesticks go, either. Even if you follow your system very, very strictly, there is still a certain percentage of being a loser, but it's not about right or wrong. If you lose, it's not because you are wrong. It is just a matter of probability.

This is how you deal with losing trades and your beliefs in trading. Every endeavor has its problems and the solution to them. The difficulty lies in your willingness and discipline to follow the rules and avoid problems.

We will dig deeper into trade management at the end of the book, which covers a lot more about elements that help you to become a better trader.

In the following chapters, I will reveal many effective systems suitable for trading an asset like cryptocurrency. Make sure to write them down and stick them on the wall beside your laptop. The heavy lifting has been done for you.

Keep It Simple

Good trading should be simple. Every seasoned trader knows this.

Nobody wants to make things complicated in life, let alone trading, where the difference between making and losing money is tiny.

But what does "keep it simple" mean? Should we only use one indicator, or say no to all indicators and base decisions on pure price action only?

From my perspective, "keep it simple" means not doing too many things at a time. In other words, you define clearly the ONE THING to do at a particular time, so that you are not overwhelmed by a lot of market signals as well as related information. In short, by keeping your trading simple, you save time while increasing the efficiency of your trading.

Below is the breakdown of the simplicity when executing a trade:

• The setup

Setup is the first indication of a trade. In a volatile market like cryptocurrency, you must filter out false or irrelevant signals that can lead to losing trades. After all, this book is specifically designed on how to avoid false signals on the trading chart. We'll explore this deeply in Chapters 6 through 9.

A setup is a set of conditions on the chart that indicate that a trade may be executed and bring potential profits. Traders may have different trade setups, depending on how they read the chart, their risk tolerance, their favorite trading time frames and size, and more.

For example, you could be a fan of breakouts from triangles and you might only execute trades within two hours after lunch.

The triangle patterns are your trade setups. When a triangle is present, it indicates that a trade "may" happen. Until the triangle appears, you should relax and do not force yourself to seek any signals. You should not be concerned about which direction the price may go, or how the news would affect the price. All you need is to clearly define a trade setup.

This is the benefit of simplicity in trading. It frees you from unnecessary thoughts and analysis paralysis.

• The triggers

Once you identify a trade setup, the next thing to consider is when to enter the trade. If a triangle appears, you know an entry may be imminent.

A trigger is a "valid occurrence" following the trade setup that suggests it's time to open a position. In the case of triangle trading, a trigger is a breakout from the triangle with a momentum/directional candlestick and its body is mostly outside the triangle. I will discuss these technical analyses later in this book. For now, this illustrates one type of trigger that you may find in your trading endeavor.

As I mentioned above, to keep your trading simple, only do one task at a time. Once you have identified a trade setup, you only need to decide what an appropriate trigger is to open your position. Simple as that.

- The exit

Exiting a trade is one of the most important tasks in trading – much more crucial than entering a trade. Hence, it is important to have in mind your potential target. Greed and fear may affect you at any time, negatively affecting your exit decisions.

Let's say you enter the trade following a breakout, and your profit target is the next resistance level. This is where you are satisfied with your profits. You would exit the trade no matter how much further the prices go.

The art of exiting a trade in crypto trading involves writing down some crystal-clear guidelines that can help you with your exit decision.

- Simple plan

Above all, simplicity in trading must have a straightforward trading plan. Unless each component in your trading plan is simple enough, it may take time to make decisions.

Your setup and trigger should be simple. Having a lot of indicators on the trading charts to define a trade setup or trigger may be counter-productive because you will have to pay attention to too many signals, which would confuse your trading decision process

In crypto trading, I focus on only a few indicators, which I will describe in the following chapters. My analysis is mainly based on price actions, and indicators are more suitable for confirmation purposes. By simplicity, I won't say you should only use the indicators described in this book. Yet, you should always keep in mind that simplicity is key.

Note: In real trading, you may not always find a 100 percent correct trade setup and trigger according to your trading plan or system. Don't worry! You may "switch" a little bit so that you won't miss many opportunities in the market.

To sum up, simplicity in trading involves a clear system that you can refer to when looking for entry and exit points. You need to look for a reliable trade setup, define a trigger that puts the odds in your favor, determine an exit (a price target for exiting the trade, and a stop-loss). Also, always try to keep the chart as clean as possible (without too many indicators on it). You only have a couple of inputs to think about, and just pay attention to just one element at a time.

This is how important simplicity is in cryptocurrency trading and investing.

Chapter 5: Indispensable Trading Ingredients

Applying the best techniques in cryptocurrency trading entails grasping the big picture of the market correctly. The art of analyzing the market includes defining the upcoming market movements, the correlation between crypto trading groups, so you can see which groups have a better chance of advancement in the (near) future.

In this chapter, I will discuss some necessary elements to help you get a better understanding of the market, thereby letting you make better decisions.

Volatility, trends, and more

First, let's talk about market volatility. Volatility describes the changes in the price of an asset, either stock, commodities, crypto, etc. It can be healthy with a steady increase or decrease, or extreme with sudden changes in price over a short period. The extreme – or high – volatility may put traders and investors in danger if they do not understand market behaviors.

Extreme volatility is often connected with market chaos, inversed direction, and loss. When the price moves between extreme highs and extreme lows, traders or investors may put more bets into its next movement, causing the price to fluctuate even more.

As for the cryptocurrency market, many consider it to be extreme, if not the most extreme, market compared to others. Trading crypto entails diligent analysis to make the best use of price movements.

Unlike other assets, there is no gauge to measure the crypto volatility. The best way to understand such volatility is by watching the charts over time to see how peaks and troughs are formed. In 2016, Bitcoin's price increased by 125% and this was considered a substantial rise. However, at the end of 2017, the advancement was at a much higher percentage, approximately 2000%, before experiencing a drastic drop of more than 50% in early 2018. In 2021, Bitcoin once again set a new all-time high, more than tripling the record made in 2017.

The frequent changes in the crypto prices make it imperative for any trader to analyze the trend or phases correctly. Before picking any setup in the market, you need to grasp what the market is telling you first.

Follow the trend until it bends

We cannot guess which way the market will go. "Follow the trend until it bends" will better secure you in a sea of fluctuations and uncertainties.

Instead of guessing which way the market will go, it is better to wait for the market to have an established trend, then you simply jump on board and follow the trend. Therefore, the best time to open a position is in the beginning of the trend. Bear in mind that you should enter the trade early, but not too early.

Trend trading makes it easier for traders to manage their trades. By identifying the trend correctly and joining the trade during the early stage, you will find it easier to manage your trade afterward. Your micro-management will be less stressful because you are stacking the odds in your favor.

By "following the trend until it bends", we will cover two aspects in trend trading:

Trend continuation: We'll discover the art of trend continuation so that we enjoy the benefits of going with the dominant side in the market.

Reversal trading - stop following the trend when it comes to an end: Identifying the end of the trend saves us from going against the new prevailing trend. "Follow the trend" doesn't mean we say NO to reversal trading, but in contrast, as you'll see in a lot of examples of reversal trading in this book, we stand a good chance of defining a new trend and start jumping on board with that new trend during its early stage.

Switch to a longer time frame first

One of the biggest oversights among traders in financial trading is they jump right to short timeframes to look for an entry price. When doing this, they may not only ignore a big picture of the market but can get lost in the weeds when developing and applying their strategies.

A seasoned trader would prefer to start their day by looking at a longer timeframe first, either a monthly or a weekly chart. Grasping the overall trend of the market helps traders succeed with their trading decisions under each circumstance. Shorter time frames are better used in identifying trade setups and triggers. We call this multi-timeframe trading.

Multi-timeframe trading is the process of viewing the price fluctuations of an asset under multiple timeframes. For example, a swing trader may choose the monthly or weekly charts in determining the long-term trend of an asset, and then switch to the daily chart and 4-hour chart for identifying the trade setup and trigger.

The optimal timeframes for each trader depend on which type of trader he/she is. For example, a day trader would not care about the monthly chart. As they tend to open and exit trades within the day, the 30-minute chart, 1-hour chart, and 4-hour chart would be the most important to them.

Take a look at this example below so you can better understand the role of multi-timeframe observation.

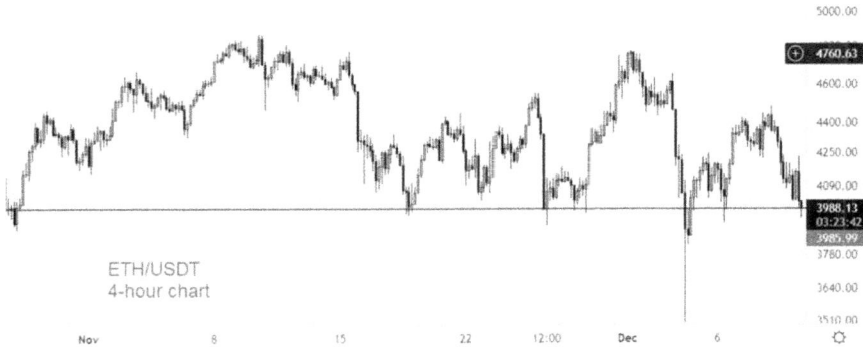

This is the Ethereum/Tether USD (ETH/USDT) chart in December 2021. At first glance, you may think the trend is in a sideways range, and you would buy bottoms and sell tops. However, when looking at the weekly chart, things are much different.

ETH/USDT
Weekly chart

Key level

Uptrend

A very strong uptrend has been in place in the year 2021. Now, the market is trying to find another low in its uptrend. Also, the price is at a key level on a weekly chart. This is when traders should look at price fluctuations carefully before deciding on an appropriate trading strategy.

In crypto trading, here are a few things you should pay attention to in multi-timeframe trading:

A bigger view: Always refer to at least one longer time frame (ideally two) other than the ones you use for identifying trade setups and triggers. In the following chapters, we'll learn a lot of techniques and strategies, but before applying any of them, just make sure to start your day by looking at a longer timeframe.

Be selective: Some cryptocurrencies in the market may not be as liquid as others, meaning that some timeframes may not be useful in analysis. For example, a crypto whose price fluctuates every few days may not offer many signals on the 1-hour chart. As a trader, you should take liquidity and your trading style into consideration in choosing the right crypto assets.

Elliott Waves: It Tells You Where Price May Go

Apart from the traditional trend determination using highs and lows which I talked a lot about in my previous books (and we'll discuss a lot in the subsequent chapters here, too), Elliott Wave is what I use frequently to define which phases the market is going through. In the following section, I will briefly show you what Elliott Waves are and how it can help us with identifying the market trend.

Elliott Wave Theory was developed in the 1930s by Ralph Nelson Elliott to reflect the market's behaviors in different phases. The main idea of this theory is the market prices move in repeatable and recognizable patterns over time. Elliott Wave is all about the trend, including five waves in the dominant trends (motive ones) and three countertrend waves (corrective ones).

Based on the structure of a trend, traders and investors can use the Elliott Wave principle to time their entry by identifying whether any price fluctuation is the continuation or the correction of a trend. An ideal price timing will be at the end of the second phase or the fourth phase.

Elliott described market moves as "waves". Take a look at a basic Elliott Wave pattern below:

Basic Elliott Wave Pattern

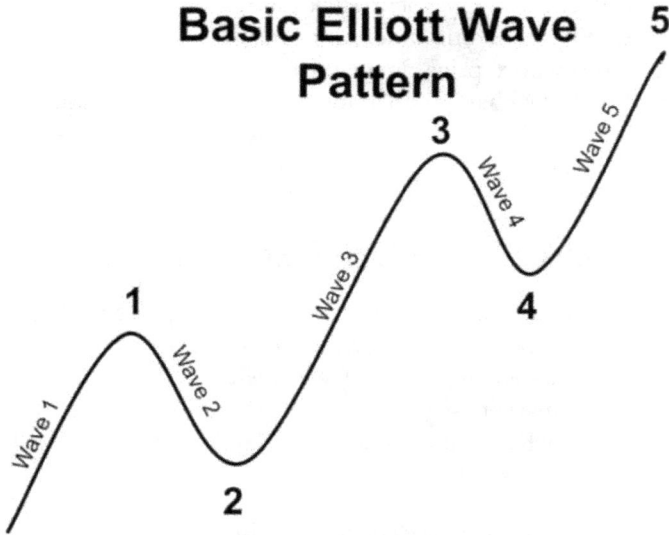

1

Wave 1

Wave 2

2

Wave 3

3

Wave 4

4

Wave 5

5

Source: bybit.com

In this picture, each mini-trend is called a wave, creating the five waves during an uptrend. The wave that starts from the left and progresses higher to "1" is Wave 1. The next wave is called Wave 2, and on, and on.

Now, let's look at a complete Elliott Wave cycle below.

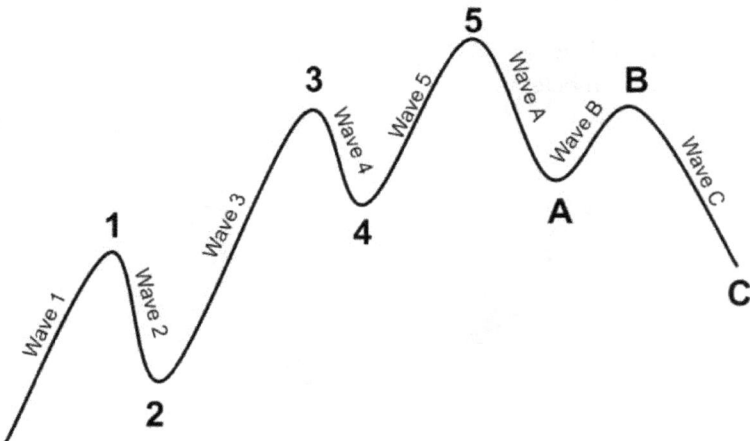

1

Wave 1

Wave 2

2

Wave 3

3

Wave 4

4

Wave 5

5

Wave A

A

Wave B

B

Wave C

C

Source: bybit.com

A complete cycle includes two types of phases, including "motive phases" – normally known as progress phase, and "corrective phases". The former is labeled with numbers while the latter is labeled with letters. Hence, a complete Elliott cycle includes eight phases in total

Identifying the Crypto trends

These Elliott Waves are beneficial in all financial markets and are widely used in the crypto market as well.

• Motive Phase

The motive phase moves with the overall trend in the market. Its goal is to progress. Moreover, this phase is thought to have five sub-waves inside. The two most popular patterns in motive waves are the impulse and diagonal ones. Take a look at the image below.

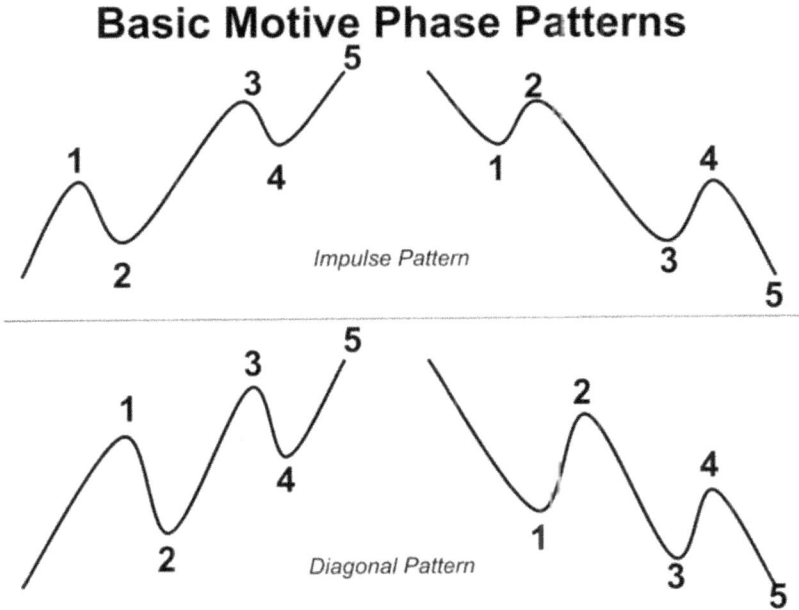

Source: bybit.com

Out of the two patterns above, the impulse pattern is the more commonly spotted one. Among the five Waves, Wave 1, 3, and 5 are impulsive ones while Wave 2 and 4 are corrective ones.

Corrective Waves within the Motive Phase

The corrective wave could be either a simple (including three sub-waves) or a complex one (including five sub-waves). As their names indicate, the aim of the corrective waves is to consolidate the previous trend. It is when the dominant side is recharging the energy before pushing the price back in the overall trend. Moreover, the two corrective waves could be different in terms of complexity.

Now, let's come to a Bitcoin chart to help you better capture these two types of waves within the motive phase.

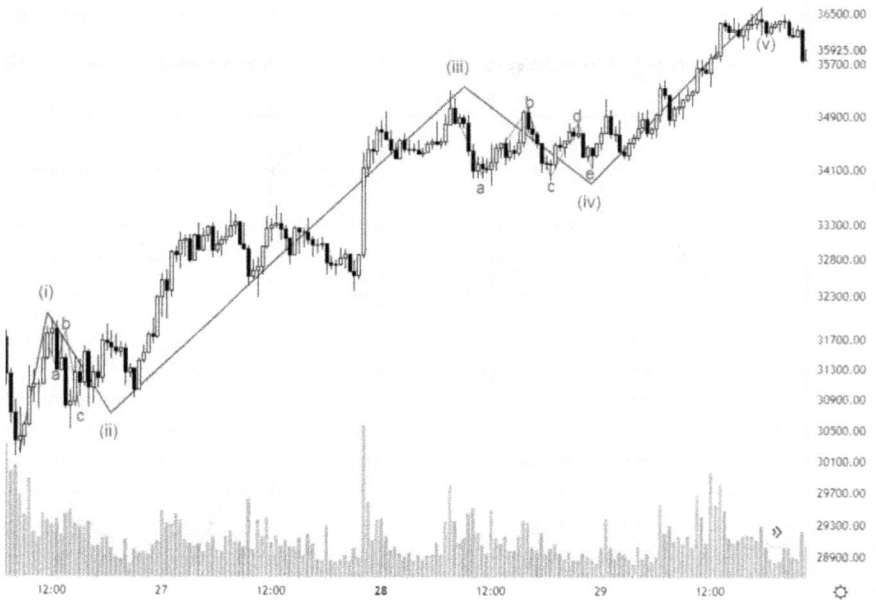

In the picture above, we see a strong uptrend of Bitcoin. Each rally is followed by a retracement before another rally appears.

The rally consists of five standard Elliott Waves as marked by Roman numerals. Notice the first corrective wave consists of three sub-waves (a simple correction) while the second corrective wave is a more complex one with five sub-waves (a complex correction).

The Depth of Corrective Waves

Following the discovery of the market structure using Elliott Wave theory, there are some rules that the market tends to respect. Some of the rules in the Elliott Wave principle focus on the depth of the corrective waves after an impulse.

As I mentioned above, the corrections occur at the second and the fourth wave. Each of these waves can be different in its depth, hence it is crucial for you to understand them to facilitate your entries. One of the best tools I use for estimating the depth of the correction is Fibonacci Retracement. Take a look at the image below:

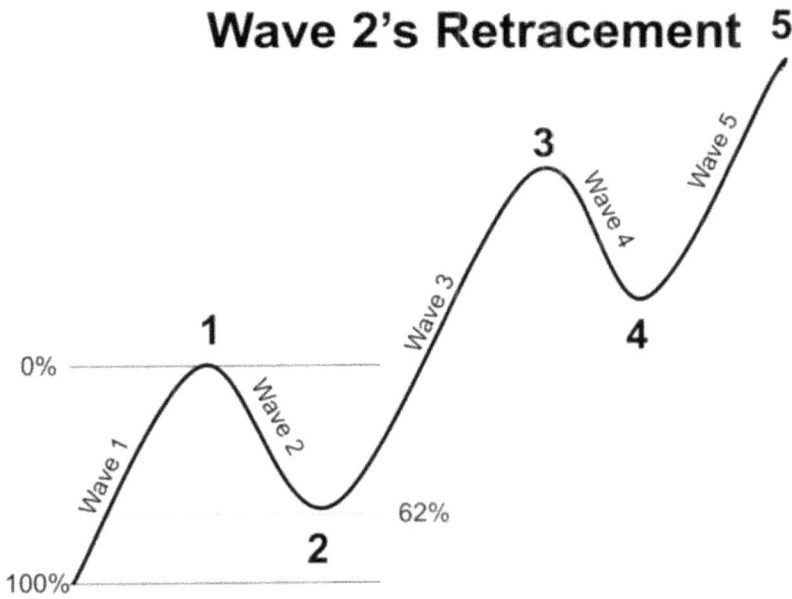

Source: bybit.com

If you believe the first wave during a motive phase has been completed, the next step is to find the depth of the correction. You know that Wave 2 must not go beyond the start of Wave 1. Using Fibonacci retracement, you will have an idea of where the retracement may end.

Accordingly, the 61.8 percent level could be targeted as a potential stop for the retracement. You might find a deeper correction at 78.6 percent or a shallower one at 50 percent. The minimum correction is the 23.6 percent area, but chances are low because Wave 2 tends to be a deeper correction compared to Wave 4.

Concerning Wave 4, it is often a shallow correction after Wave 3 (normally the longest wave) is completed. A retracement around the 23.6 percent level or the 38.2 percent level is where to look for the end of the correction.

• Corrective Phase

After the fifth wave in the Motive Phase, the market can form a substantial correction called the Corrective Phase, which would fall into one of the three patterns below.

Basic Corrective Phase Patterns

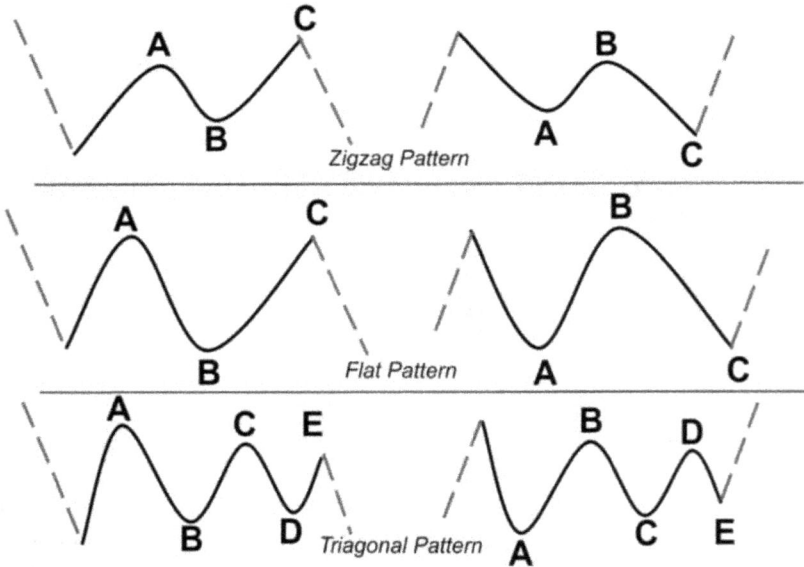

Source: bybit.com

Detailed Example of Elliott Waves Application

Take a look at the Ethereum chart below where the price formed the first two waves during the motive phase in March 2021.

As you can see, Wave (I) is an impulse wave, which consists of five sub-waves. Wave (II) is a corrective wave (a zigzag one), which corrects near the 61.8 percent Fibonacci retracement level.

Now, let's see how the rally continues:

Again, we can easily identify Wave 3, which consists of five sub-waves. Contrary to Wave 2, Wave 4 is a complex triagonal pattern, ending near the 38.2 percent Fibonacci level of Wave 3. From there, Ethereum continues its rally to the fifth wave.

Elliott Wave and the Art of Trend Trading

As our goal in cryptocurrency trading is to spot a trend during its early stage, Elliott Wave can be a great tool to help you achieve this. Within the Elliott Wave cycle, there are certain waves that can help you ride the wave better than others. Defining a wave successfully using the Elliott Wave cycle puts you in a better position to apply strategies (more on that in the following chapters) and reduce the risks.

You know that Wave 3 is often the longest one, hence it is advisable to determine the end of Wave 2 so that you can join the trade during the beginning of Wave 3 in the Cycle. It is what most traders always long for in riding the wave.

Wave 5 could also be a good option to trade, first by assessing the end of Wave 4.

Sometimes, Wave A and Wave C during a correction could also be traded if you aim to reap a quick profit thanks to short-term price fluctuations. Whereas, if you are a long-term trader, trading these waves may not be of great interest due to their narrower movement magnitude.

Elliott Wave is a perfect tool for anyone who aims to spot the prevailing trend and waves in the market. It's not surprising why seasoned traders are constantly talking about "what wave they are in".

Bitcoin and Altcoin Correlation: Why Pro Traders Always Pay Attention To This

Another way to put you in a position to find a trade setup is through analyzing the correlation between Bitcoin and Altcoins.

Bitcoin Dominance: The Power Of the Giant

Bitcoin Dominance is an index that reflects how much Bitcoin takes out of the total cryptocurrency market capitalization. The maximum index is 100 (percent), and the minimum index is 0 (percent).

The most noticeable thing about the Bitcoin Dominance index is that it tells you about the correlation between Bitcoin and Altcoins.

If the Bitcoin Dominance goes up, Altcoins, in general, loses value against Bitcoin.

If the Bitcoin Dominance goes down, Altcoins, in general, gains value against Bitcoin.

In other words, if the Bitcoin Dominance chart suggests that the index tends to go up, you would want to be in Bitcoin. On the other hand, you would transfer more money to Altcoins if Bitcoin Dominance is in a downtrend. In most cases, a steep downtrend in Bitcoin Dominance occurs in crypto bull markets, because Altcoins capitalization tends to increase at a higher speed than Bitcoin during a bull market. Meanwhile, a correction of this trend might be the indication of a bear market.

Price Correlation – Indispensable mutual relationships

On the whole, Bitcoin price affects Altcoins to some extent. The relationship is not 100 percent correct in every circumstance, yet it does give you good ideas in many cases.

We have all known that Bitcoin is the primary cryptocurrency in the crypto market. It is Altcoins that fund the Bitcoin movement and vice versa. Hence, there are certain correlations between the price of Bitcoin and Altcoins. Below are some points to note:

- BTC price gradually rises > Altcoins in run -> money poured into Altcoins

- BTC price runs → Altcoins can either drop or increase over Bitcoin → it depends on each circumstance to decide where we should be.

- BTC price drops → most Altcoins will drop, even harder than BTC → be in dollars

Now, let's dig a little bit deeper into each scenario.

When Bitcoin skyrocket, it may:

- Suppresses Altcoins because money is poured into Bitcoin (Altcoins may hold their value in dollar but lose value against Bitcoin).

- Push Altcoins higher as well (higher possibility). This is the perfect scenario for crypto traders. From my experience, in a dominant bull market, some Altcoins in the top 20 may increase stronger than Bitcoin.

When Bitcoin plummets, it may:

- Cause Altcoins to fall as well because money is transferred into fiat currency (higher possibility). This is the least favorable scenario for bull traders.

- Cause Altcoins to boom as traders sell Bitcoin and buy Altcoins. It is when some Altcoins are advertised to be "the next Bitcoin". Be cautious during these times when scammers are everywhere.

When Bitcoin price is stagnant, it may:

• Cause the Altcoins to stagnate or fall. This is a common situation when Bitcoin is sitting around a support or resistance zone.

• Cause Altcoins to boom as people believe in greater return with Altcoins. This is the number one scenario for Altcoin traders to trade short-term. You are most likely to see this situation when BTC is forming a bottom after a fall or is consolidating after a rally.

From my observation, the condition where most cryptos are stagnant is ideal for some breakout patterns to form (triangle, flat, etc.). This is when a trigger is imminent. In Chapter 7, you will learn how to make the most out of this type of trading.

All in all, it is most advisable to play with Altcoins when Bitcoin is stagnant. Meanwhile, the worst case to bet with Altcoins is when Bitcoin is dropping.

To summarize, since Bitcoin has been the core of the crypto market for many years, its gravity on the Altcoins' price is undeniable. There will be times when you will find it hard to analyze crypto's next movements on the chart. These are the times you should refer to the above theories. Although they are not always true, they can help us in many circumstances.

In the next four chapters, we'll explore powerful cryptocurrency trading strategies in detail.

Chapter 6: Candlestick and Support/Resistance Decoded

Support & Resistance - The Basis For Everything Else

From this chapter onward, support/resistance is the basis for nearly every strategy we explore. Support/resistance is one of the most frequently discussed topics in technical analysis. We'll discuss many types of support/resistance in this book, both manually depicted and indicator-based. But first, let's look at a simple definition of support/resistance.

Support and Resistance Defined

Support is a price zone or level which attracts buying interest, thus causing a downtrend to pause for some time. When any crypto decreases in price, demand for it goes up, forming the support zone, where the bulls are waiting to jump on board.

Conversely, resistance is a price zone that attracts selling interest, causing an uptrend to pause for a while before finding the next direction. The higher the price is, the more crypto holders want to sell, forming a resistance zone/level.

Now, let's take a look at support/resistance levels.

In this Bitcoin chart, notice how the price touches the $48,500 level several times without breaking through it. In this case, the $48,500 level is the resistance level. It acts as a ceiling where the price tends to bounce back when touching. It is not until the resistance is broken that traders can expect a strong upward move.

Still on the same chart, if you look at the bottom, the $41,000 price level acts as a floor which the price bounces back every time it touches. This zone prevents the price from going down further, and buyers come in to fuel the price rise each time the price approaches the level.

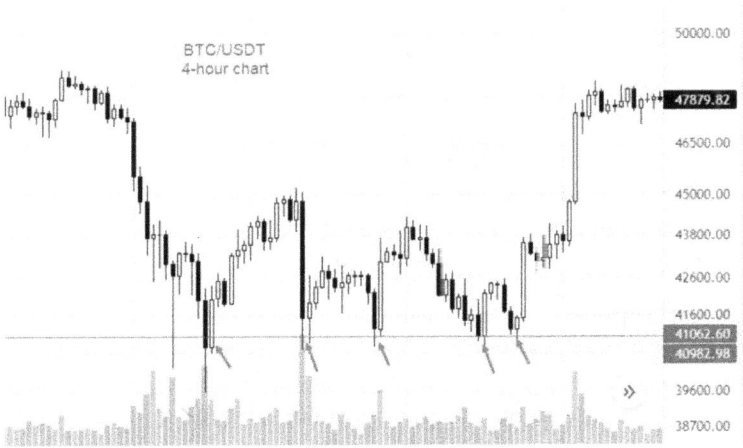

A support/resistance zone can be a potential area to look for a trade setup and trigger. When the price touches a key level, it can either bounce back or poke through it. Trading in the direction of the price reaction can reduce risks involved and brings about a potentially good risk-reward ratio.

Also, support/resistance is ideal for a profit-taking target. This is where the dominant side may show certain exhaustion, and exiting a trade at the next support/ resistance level will never be a bad idea. Keep that in mind.

Round number

Another noticeable characteristic of support/ resistance level is that the price may have difficulty pushing through a round number price. Take a look at the picture below to see how Bitcoin had difficult times breaking through the $40,000 level.

BTC/USDT
4-hour chart

One explanation for this is that price targets or stop orders set by both whales and retail traders are often located at a round number price level. When a lot of orders are placed at the same level, that level tends to act as a point where sellers and buyers meet, forming support/resistance.

Note: Support/resistance can come in various forms. In this chapter, I am referring to the horizontal/ vertical lines. In Chapter 7 and Chapter 9, I will discuss two other types of support/resistance levels that I use not only in crypto trading but also in other types of trading as well.

Are you drawing support & resistance correctly?

Drawing support/resistance correctly is unquestionably the most important aspect in trading successfully in the financial markets. In this section, we'll learn how to draw support and resistance levels correctly so they would not become counterproductive in your trading.

A common mistake many traders make is they use too many lines on the charts and don't know which one is more important than others, and which one they should focus more on for identifying potential trade opportunities. Below is a typical example of key levels which might make you confused.

BTC/USDT
4-hour chart

By drawing many horizontal lines in a chart likes this, you'll not be able to focus on the most important and relevant ones on the chart. In the sections below, I will reveal the most important criteria in drawing support/resistance.

- The support/resistance levels reject the price multiple times (ideally three rejections or more);

Take a look at another Bitcoin chart below:

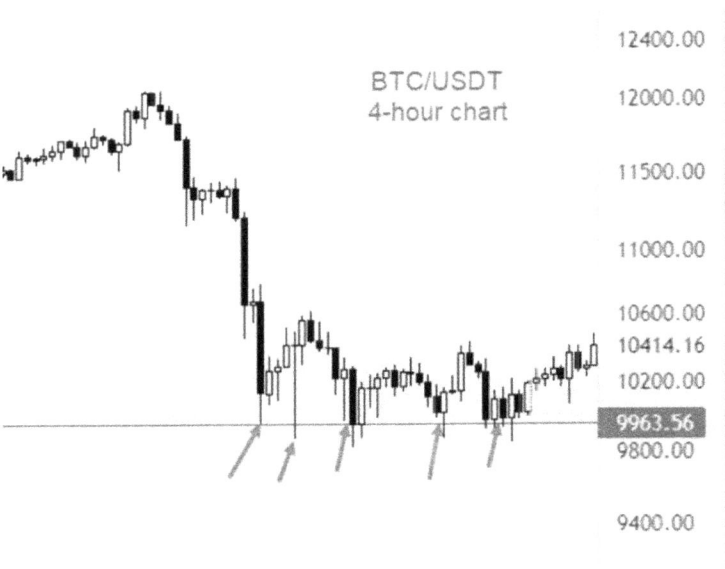

BTC/USDT
4-hour chart

In this chart, the $9,963 level proves to be a strong support level by rejecting candlesticks multiple times. Hence, this level meets the first condition of valid support to take into consideration in trading.

The more rejection a support/resistance level makes, the stronger it is. It would be ideal to have at least three price touches, but two may often work in some cases, depending on some other criteria presented next below.

- Drastic bounce from swing high/low:

A strong support/resistance is where the price bounces back considerably after hitting. Look at the 52,777$ Bitcoin price level on the chart. We can see there is no prior rejection at this level recently. However, when the price hits this price zone from the first time, it falls drastically to 40,000$ price level, a drop of more than 20% in value. Hence, it can also be considered a strong resistance level.

- Support can be resistance, and vice versa (not a compulsory condition, but it's my preferred trading technique)

This is one characteristic of how support and resistance work in the financial market in general and the crypto market in particular. Take a look at the 4-hour Litecoin/Tether USD (LTC/USDT) chart below.

To the left of the chart, the price has some difficulties breaking through the $164 level. After some attempts, the price eventually broke the level, opening the way for higher advancements. Yet, it does not make a rally right away. Instead, the price revisits the $164 level, which now acts as a support level, a few times. In this case, the former resistance line has become a support line.

- The level must be close to the current price.

This is a "must-have" condition that few traders pay attention to. Ignoring this criterion may result in multiple horizontal support and resistance levels on the chart, which is both unnecessary and confusing.

BNB/USDT
4-hour chart

1

2

3

4

5

647.2
614.5
01:34
580.0
560.0
540.0
527.2
520.0
500.0
488.5
480.0
460.0
446.9
429.0
413.0
397.9

In this chart, the current price of Binance (the third most traded cryptocurrency at the time of writing) is $614. As you can see, I draw five key levels from the top to the bottom. They are marked (1), (2), (3), (4) and (5) and are located at $657, $527, $488, $447, and $397 price levels respectively. However, for proper support/resistance displaying, we only need the first two lines, which are close to the current Binance price level. Regarding the three remaining levels, they are not directly involved in determining the next price action on the chart, hence it is better to remove them from the trading chart.

With this discussed, I don't mean the key levels (3), (4), and (5) are useless. What I mean is you should ignore them at least until the price breaks below the key level (2). By doing this, your trading chart will be much cleaner.

Now, we have the full set of criteria in determining support/resistance effectively. Let's look at the Ethereum chart below which represents a perfect support/resistance level on the chart.

Notice there are three key levels on the chart, and the current price is $4,417.

Starting from the top, we can spot the first key level at $4,800. You can see how the price makes a dramatic swing high to this price level and then drops drastically to the $4,000 level. Hence, it satisfies the first criterion of price bouncing back strongly from a key level. Next, it is located near the current price, which satisfies the second criterion of the rules. We're done. This is the first validated resistance on the chart.

Moving downward to the middle of the chart, where a key level at $4,000 is drawn. Let's see which criteria this price level satisfies.

First, there are multiple rejections at the 4,000 level. Second, it was formerly a resistance level before becoming a support level recently. Next, this level is also close to the current price. These three conditions are more than enough to confirm that this is a key level that traders need to pay close attention to.

We can also see the third level at the price of $2,800 (the dotted one). Although the price moves drastically from this, it is located too far from the current price. This is why I don't confirm it to be a key level to draw on the chart.

Before going deeper into trading with candlestick patterns, here are some points you need to know when using support/resistance levels:

You don't need to gather every criterion above in confirming support or resistance that is valid. Sometimes, only two conditions are enough. Yet, as I always say, the more, the better.

The support/resistance presented in this chapter as well as the following chapters should be treated as zones or areas instead of the exact price level. You might see I use the word "level" more often, yet you should understand it as a zone, which allows for a certain tolerance without reflecting market fluctuations incorrectly.

By only drawing support and resistance levels that directly affect your next trading decision and ignoring the ones that don't, you make your trading much easier and more efficient. In the next sections, I will show you strategies based on a perfect combination between candlestick patterns and support/resistance levels.

Engulfing pattern

The first candlestick pattern that I am going to cover in this chapter is the engulfing pattern.

An engulfing pattern is commonly spotted when a trend is about to end and the opposite trend starts. In other words, engulfing patterns are most used in reversal trading. A typical example of this pattern includes two candlesticks, in which the second candlestick moves in an opposite direction of the previous one and engulfs that candlestick. An engulfing pattern can appear both in an uptrend and a downtrend. Let's look at a visual illustration of a bullish engulfing pattern below:

Bullish candle

Bearish candle

Open

Close

Gap lower

Bullish candle closes above previous candle's open

The length of the bullish candle engulfs the previous bearish candle

Bullish candle opens at, or lower than the previous candle's close

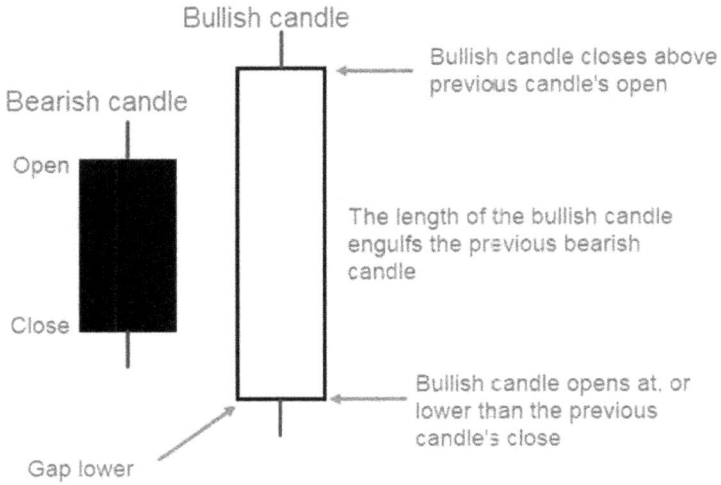

While an engulfing candlestick may signal a potential trend reversal, you cannot open a position just because it appears. Trading this way could put traders in great danger. This brings us to the first technique in trading with support/resistance:

Principle:

- Identify key support/resistance level(s).

- Look for an engulfing pattern on one of the key levels. (Would be ideal if the engulfing candlestick body is longer than most of the previous ones).

- Set entry price, stop-loss, and take-profit levels.

Look at the Ethereum daily chart below:

In this chart, we have a support level of $1,781. Starting from the left of the chart, the price fell strongly to this support zone before shooting up drastically, making it key support on the chart. After some time, when price revisited the level again before starting a huge rally. But here are some good points to note.

Notice that on the way to the support level for the second time, the bearish candlesticks were getting smaller and smaller, indicating a momentum loss of the sellers.

Moreover, a bullish candlestick appeared at this support level, totally engulfing the previous candlestick. It is the ideal engulfing pattern we are looking for. It tells us that sellers tried to push the price below the support level for some time, but they encountered strong force from the buyers, causing the price to advance higher than the latest bearish candlestick during the downtrend.

A trade entry can be placed at the close of the engulfing pattern, with the stop loss just below the support level. Starting from the key support level, the market has no difficulty in spectacularly doubling within two months. This is how crazy cryptocurrencies go in many cases.

Let's look at another engulfing pattern on a key resistance level.

In this 4-hour Bitcoin/Tether USD (BTC/USDT) chart, the price approaches the $19,400 level several times but was rejected by the level. We can see there are two fake-outs along the way when the price attempted to break through the key resistance level but encountered pressure from the sellers and reversed back below the key zone. Finally, a bearish candlestick appears at the exact 19,400 price level, fully engulfing the previous candlestick. At that time, the sellers keep coming in, aggressively pulling the price downward.

This is one of the most ideal situations to open a trade with the confirmation of a resistance level and an engulfing candlestick. We will investigate more about it in the next section, but at this moment, you can be confident of the strength in combining two of the most powerful trade patterns in financial trading.

Key takeaways:

- Never trade an engulfing pattern unless it appears on a (key) support/ resistance level.

- The bigger the engulfing candlestick body is, the better.

Rejection Pattern

Rejection candlestick – commonly known as pin bar candlestick, indicates a transformation of the strength or power from the sellers to the buyers, and vice versa. It suggests a sharp reversal or price rejection. A typical pin bar candlestick includes a long tail (or "shadow", "wick") and a small body, which is the difference between the open price and close price of a candlestick.

Have a look at the picture below:

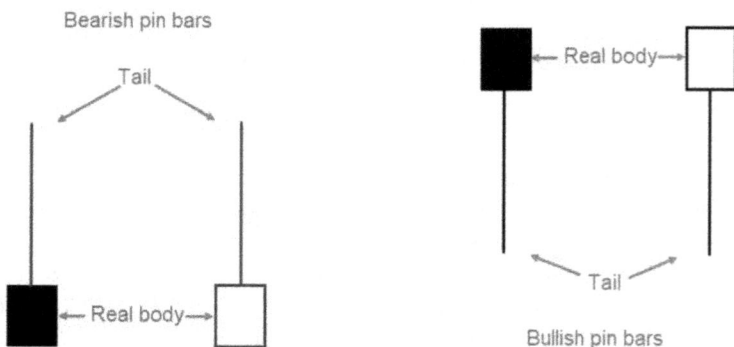

The length of the tail in a pin bar candlestick indicates how the price is rejected and implies that the price may go in the opposite direction of the tail point. For example, a bearish pin bar with a long upper tail suggests the price is more likely to fall soon.

Whereas, a bullish pin bar with a long lower tail demonstrates how difficult it is for the price to go downward. In this case, the pin bar may signal a bullish move afterward.

With that said, I have to make a big "warning" that you should not trade any pin bar just because it appears. Without seeking other price action confirmations, you are likely to lose money after all.

Principle:

- Identify key support/resistance level(s);

- Look for a rejection pattern on one of the key levels (would be ideal if the rejection candlestick has a short body and a longer shadow than most of the previous candlesticks);

- Set entry price, stop-loss, and take-profit levels.

Now, let's move to an example to see how it works:

ETH/USDT
4-hour chart

rejection candlestick

4900.00
4800.00
4678.29
13:47
4600.00
4500.00
4400.00
4300.00
4220.00
4140.00
4060.00
3987.66
3910.00

If you followed me until now, you will see the zone around $4,000 is a super strong support level in the Ethereum price chart. The above picture was captured at the time of writing.

First, to the left of the chart, notice the price bounces back several times when touching the $4,000 price level. When we look at the right of the chart, after revisiting the level, the price establishes a bullish price rejection formation. This candle has a small body while its shadow is longer than that of several candlesticks before. This signals that at one point, sellers were strong and tried to take the price toward the key support zone, however, they could not fight against aggressive buyers at this level, and the price shot up from the strong upside momentum of the market.

If you are unsure about the pin bar candlestick and need one more reliable signal, the next candlestick after that is typically a directional candlestick with a long body and barely has any shadow (known as "marubozu"). It further confirms that the buyers are dominating the battle at that moment.

Depending on the degree of your risk tolerance, you may choose to enter the trade at the close of the rejection candlestick or the close of the directional candlestick. To me, a rejection candlestick located at a key level is often worth trying an entry order.

Let's look at another example with a reversal from the uptrend to the downtrend.

In this Avalanche/ Tether USD (AVAX/USDT) 4-hour chart, let's focus on the resistance level at $50.23. The price approached it a few times in the past, including one occasion where it made a drastic downward move from the resistance. The difficulties in breaking the resistance zone to the upside continued, and finally, a rejection candlestick pattern formed. This candlestick has a very little body and a long wick, indicating that the buyers did try to push the price above the resistance at one time, but the bears came in and easily outshined the bulls.

From the rejection pattern, the price fell dramatically, and those who entered a short position at the resistance would profit.

Similar to engulfing pattern trading, a trade entry could be placed at the close of the rejection candlestick. The stop-loss could be placed either above the highest point of the pattern or above the resistance level, depending on your risk tolerance.

Key takeaways:

- Never trade a rejection pattern unless it appears on a (key) support/ resistance level.

- The longer the tail and the smaller the body, the better.

Shrinking Pattern

Bullish shrinking pattern

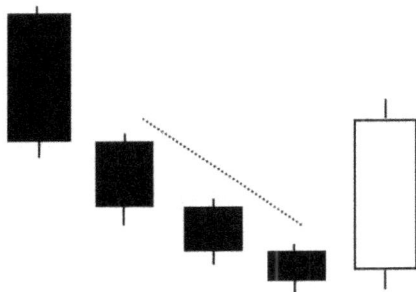

As its name implies, the bullish shrinking patterns include candles that shrink in the body successively until a strong bullish candlestick breaks above some latest shrinking ones, signaling a reversal of the trend. In theory, the shrinking cluster includes some bearish candlesticks in which each one is followed by a smaller one until a bullish candlestick breaks above the high of the cluster.

This shrinking process indicates the loss of downward momentum in the market while the strong bullish candlestick at the end of the process serves as the trigger for entering the trade (at the closing price).

Bearish shrinking pattern

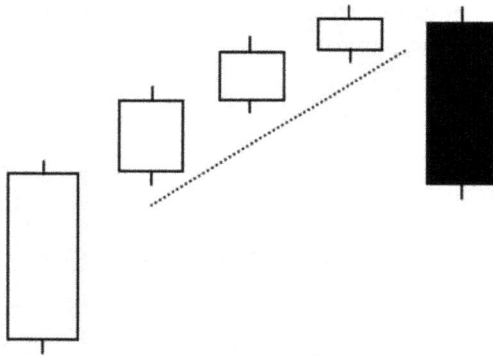

A bearish shrinking pattern is theoretically composed of some bullish candlesticks which successively shrink in their body size until a strong bearish appears and breaks through the low of the shrinking cluster (ideally consisting of three latest candlesticks), paving the way for the price to head lower and lower.

Psychologically speaking, this shrinking process indicates a loss in the upside momentum and lower volatility in the market before a bearish confirmation signal is confirmed, validating a reversal.

Shrinking patterns can be combined with other price action methods to detect the reversal of the trend. In the section about engulfing pattern trading, we can see a combination between engulfing patterns and shrinking patterns (although not a perfect example under the theory). In these examples below, I will show how to benefit from shrinking patterns displayed on key levels.

Principles:

- Identify key support/resistance level(s).

- Look for a shrinking pattern when the price approaches one of the key levels.

- Set entry price, stop-loss, and take-profit levels.

Example: Shrinking patterns on key support

First, let's look at a bigger picture of Ripple (XRP) price in early 2021 to identify a key support/resistance zone.

In this chart, a key level at $0.3567 is in place. Notice how price had difficulties breaking through it twice. On the second time, the price bounced dramatically from this level, making it a validated resistance. After several candlesticks, the price still remembered this level and revisited for the third time. The only difference is that at this time, the previous resistance flipped into support, which further confirms that this is a validated key level.

Now, let's zoom onto the price action on the third touch to see what happened.

Big bearish candlestick, followed by smaller ones

XRP/USDT
4-hour chart

After breaking the $0.3567 level, the price climbed quickly before losing its upside momentum. The bears jumped in and pulled the price back to the key level again with a huge bearish candlestick pattern. However, the sellers lost their energy on their way to the level, with the following candlesticks becoming smaller and smaller in the body as illustrated on the chart. This is the first signal that tells one pullback may happen in the near future, and traders should be prepared for a long entry.

As we can see, after successfully revisiting the support, the next candlestick is a bullish one that fully engulfed the previous candlestick. Placing a trade at the end of this candle, with a stop-loss under the key level, would bring a handsome profit.

Example: Shrinking patterns on key resistance

First, we identify key support/resistance on the 4-hour Bitcoin chart in June 2021.

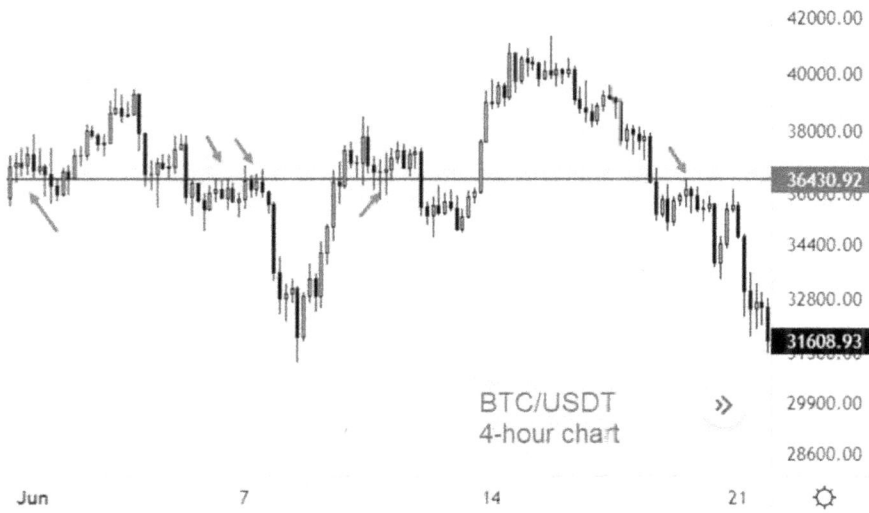

BTC/USDT
4-hour chart

Let's look at the $36,430 level which plays as both support and resistance interchangeably. Considering multiple touches within a short time period, this is a validated support/resistance level.

Now, let's see what happened next after a while.

BTC/USDT
4-hour chart

The price revisited the $36,430 level, which acted as resistance then. Notice the bullish candlesticks became smaller and smaller on their way to the resistance level, suggesting a loss of momentum in the bulls. Then, a bearish candlestick (the directional one) formed, fully engulfing the previous candlesticks on the chart, signaling an official shift of trading momentum.

Here is what happened next on the chart.

From the key level, the price fell quite smoothly from $36,430 to just above $29,100 in just three weeks, a drop of 20% in value.

Now that you have some understanding of shrinking patterns, here are some tips that will truly serve you more in trading with them.

Shrinking patterns in real trading may not perfectly align with the theory. The directional candlestick may not cover a cluster of three. For example, it may engulf only one or two previous candlesticks. However, this doesn't refute the possibility of an imminent trend reversal. In those cases, just wait for one or two more candlesticks to have a better insight into the market behaviors.

You should widen the use of shrinking patterns instead of limiting their use in identifying entry points. The best function of this pattern lies in signaling a loss of steam from buyers or sellers at a particular period. It doesn't necessarily appear on a key level, which everyone can see. Shrinking patterns can scatter somewhere distant from support/resistance. It can, however, tell traders if the market strength has some signs of shifting from buyers to sellers, and vice versa. A good trader should be able to grasp a potential shift of power before it happens. Shrinking patterns is super-powerful in helping you do that, though they don't appear as frequently as engulfing and rejection patterns.

Stop-loss Placement

We have gone over this technique when describing the entry price option. There are some options of placing a stop-loss under this trading method:

First, as I mentioned, a stop-loss under the support level or above the resistance level can be safe enough for a trade. It can be hit sometimes, but that's part of trading. This endeavor is all about probability.

If you are more conservative in your stop-loss placement, using Average True Range (ATR) is a great option. We will learn more about it in Chapter 11 about stop-loss placement and trailing. Ideally, ATR can be used for several trading methods.

Stop-loss is an indispensable element in any trade, but don't make it too complicated.

Take-profit

Profit-taking is vitally important in trading any type of asset, yet I always try to make it as simple as possible. There aren't any magic pills in setting a take-profit price for your trade. Instead, the simpler, the better. Below are two options I use most of the time.

- Next support/resistance level

When it comes to taking profit, the first price level I will think of is the next support/resistance level. Yes, this chapter is about trading with support/resistance and I can't stress enough the importance of using it in every trade I take. Keep in mind you can use the next support/resistance level as the exit price of the trade no matter which methods you use to enter the trades.

You might understand the idea behind this exit option. This is often where the opposite side jumps in the battle and the previous swing may have certain difficulties poking through a key level. While you are not sure whether the price will bounce back or break through the key levels, you should stack some profits and wait for a clear direction to join later. Simple as that.

Also, when choosing to trade using pure support/resistance and candlestick patterns, it's better to opt for a risk-reward ratio of at least 1:2 (ideally 1:3 and above). There's more on that at the end of the book when we go further into risk-reward ratio.

• Momentum loss

Another method for profit-taking is by way of a momentum loss. As I mentioned above, a loss of momentum does not necessarily happen on a key level (although it may often be so). While momentum shortage might pave the way for a possible trade entry, it can also signal the prevailing momentum is about to end and traders should be prepared for an exit. One drawback of this strategy, however, is that you need to monitor it closely to identify when a momentum shortage occurs. You cannot set a predefined exit price target as in the first method.

Recommended time frame:

Any time frame, suitable for both short-term trading and long-term investment (day trading, swing trading, long-term investment)

To summarize, you have learned the three most popular and effective candlestick pattern trading strategies in crypto trading. A key secret to use when trading these patterns, as we discussed many times, is to analyze the candlesticks' behaviors when they are at a support or resistance level. This seems easy at first, however, a successful application of these secrets entails a lot of patience.

Also, there are some types of candlestick patterns on the charts, so the candlestick techniques presented in this chapter are not exhaustive. Yet, they are the most popular ones which I use 95 percent of the time and benefit well from them.

I hope this chapter gives you a good idea of trading candlestick patterns with simplicity and effectiveness.

Chapter 7: Trend Lines Trading Explained

In the previous chapter, we've learned about horizontal support/resistance. In this chapter, we will learn one more type of support/resistance – the trend line. There are many ways and techniques to execute your trade using trend lines. Yet, trading them successfully entails certain skills and techniques which is not widely discussed out there.

In the sections below, we will reveal how I benefit from trend lines trading using simple and effective trading strategies.

What is a trend line?

A trend line is an easily recognizable line that traders can draw on the chart to connect a series of highs or lows. The line is used to give traders a good idea of the current direction of the market price. The trend is your friend until it bends, hence defining the trend is the very first step in any trading process.

As I mentioned above, a trend line is a visual representation of support and resistance across different time frames. Moreover, the slope of the line can be a good reflection of how quickly the price increases or decreases.

To draw a trend line, we need at least two points on the chart to connect. Some prefer using it on a long timeframe such as monthly, week, or daily chart while others prefer shorter time frames such as five-minute or fifteen-minute charts. For better trend analysis, you should start drawing trend lines from a longer time frame (e.g monthly or weekly ones) so that it can give you a clearer overall picture of the market behaviors first.

Let's look at a trend line example below:

BTC/USDT
Daily chart

In this example, you can easily spot a bullish trend line where the price tends to bounce upward when it hits the line.

There can be two trend lines that keep the price within a range, also called a consolidation period. Those two trend lines are where some types of widely known breakout patterns form. I will describe this in more detail in the next sections of this chapter. First, take a look at an example of a consolidation made up of two lines:

Lower highs

Support

BTC/USDT
Daily chart

When it comes to trend line trading, there are two well-known trading styles.

- **Pullback Trading**: Considering financial trading in general and crypto trading in particular, the market never goes straight up or down for a sustained period. Instead, it may take a rest along the way where no clear direction is spotted. This is when the dominating side recharges its energy before bouncing back from the trend line and going with the original trend. Pullback trading has more to do with the trend continuation.

- **Breakout trading**: Similar to pullback trading, breakout trading originates from a consolidation period where the prevailing side takes a rest and regains its steam along the way. But unlike the former, breakout trading can be used in both trend continuation and trend reversal circumstances (though more popular with trend continuation). Traders would wait for the price to break either above or below a trend line or a consolidation area and consider trading in the direction of the breakout.

Again, just because the price hits the trend line does not guarantee the price will change its direction or bounce back. I will discuss later how to analyze the price action occurring at a trend line.

Before that, let's learn about how to draw a trend line the right way.

Secrets of drawing a trend line

Drawing a trend line correctly may not be an easy task for a new trader. Incorrectly displaying a trend line can result in more confusion than benefits, including a lot of annoying adjustments to the line to fit several price actions. In the section below, I will show you a simple method for drawing a trend line properly.

A common concern that many traders have lies in whether they should connect the candlestick's closing price or the wick's end. While there can be conflicting opinions to this concern, I prefer to draw it in a way that produces as many touches as possible. In other words, the more highs or lows the trend line crosses (depending on whether the line is upward or downward), the better. Have a look at the example below:

BTC/USDT
Daily chart

In this Bitcoin chart, we can easily spot an uptrend as the market is producing higher highs and higher lows. Hence, we need to connect the lows on the chart to create a trend line. Look at the way the trend line connects as many touches as possible. This may result in some candlesticks or "groups of candlesticks" overlapping of the trend line while some nearly touch the line. It's perfectly acceptable when you see these situations. Here is why:

Psychologically speaking, at some time in the financial market, many other traders (including many newbie traders who may not be patient enough) are also paying attention to the trend line, along with support and resistance level you are watching out for. When some of them see the price gradually approaching the trend line, more often than not they initiate an entry position just before the price touches the trend line, causing the price to miss the line very slightly.

On the other hand, when looking at the overlapping clusters on the chart above, you can see there aren't directional candlesticks within them. This suggests that at some point, the sellers tried to break the trend line and initiate a trend reversal, yet they were not strong enough and were easily beaten by the bulls. Considering this, some overlapping clusters or candlesticks are normal in a financial trading chart.

Also, as I mentioned above, a trend line is a visual representation of support/resistance. Hence, you should treat it as an area or zone instead of an exact line. No trend line can connect all the highs and lows perfectly. Hence, the best thing we can do is try to connect as many highs or lows as possible. Doing this, we can have a best possible picture of the market direction.

Now that you have learned how to draw the trend line in the most effective way, let's move to my favorite trading strategies using trend lines.

Trend Line Pullback Trading

Pullback trading refers to the price bouncing back to the direction of the previous trend after hitting the trend line. It is a typical example of continuation trading, in which a trend line acts as a floor or ceiling (depending on the slope of the trend line).

With that said, you should not immediately open a trade just because the price hits the line. Instead, you need other price action method(s) to confirm your analysis and decision.

If you've grasped my trading style reflected in some of my books, I never enter a trade without at least one confirmation signal. Below are the most effective signals that I often use:

Using a second trend line

A great technique that you can use as a trade confirmation is a second trend line. Let's look at the daily price fluctuations on Bitcoin/Tether USDT (BTC/USDT) in October 2021 using the chart below.

While the first trend line serves as a basis for you to watch out for a trade opportunity, the second trend is for trade trigger purposes. After the price has broken through this mini trend line, you can enter your position at the close of the breakout candlestick. Doing this, you would better put the odds in your favor because you are using two trend lines perfectly combined instead of only one line as many traders often use.

As you can see in the picture above, the price rocketed from $48,000 to nearly $68,000 (a staggering 40% increase in value) in just two weeks. You would sit on a nice profit if you chose the double trend line technique in this case.

Now, let's look at how this strategy can be applied in a downtrend.

In this Bitcoin chart, a downtrend was in place, hence we need a trend line connecting the highs. Still using the same technique, we can draw a second trend line to find a trigger for the trade. Notice that when breaking the second trend line, only a small body of the breakout candlestick is below the second line, hence we need to have one more bearish candlestick to confirm our short position.

The market then dropped from $64,000 to around $53,000, a 17% fall in value in just two weeks.

Using Stochastic Oscillator

Another indicator you can use in confirming a trend continuation is stochastic oscillator.

The stochastic oscillator is a momentum indicator developed by George C. Lane in the late 1950s to compare a particular closing price of a security to its high-low price range over a set period. The default set period number is 14, which can be calculated in days, weeks, months or an intraday time frame.

The stochastic oscillator consists of two lines, one indicating the actual value of the oscillator and the other indicating its three-day simple moving average. A cross between these lines indicates a shift of the price momentum, and traders often look for a change in the direction of the price during these times.

The stochastic oscillator is range-bound between zero and one hundred. Its main purpose is to predict the overbought and oversold areas. Any reading below 20 is considered oversold while a reading over 80 is considered overbought.

Take a look at an example below regarding stochastic oscillator:

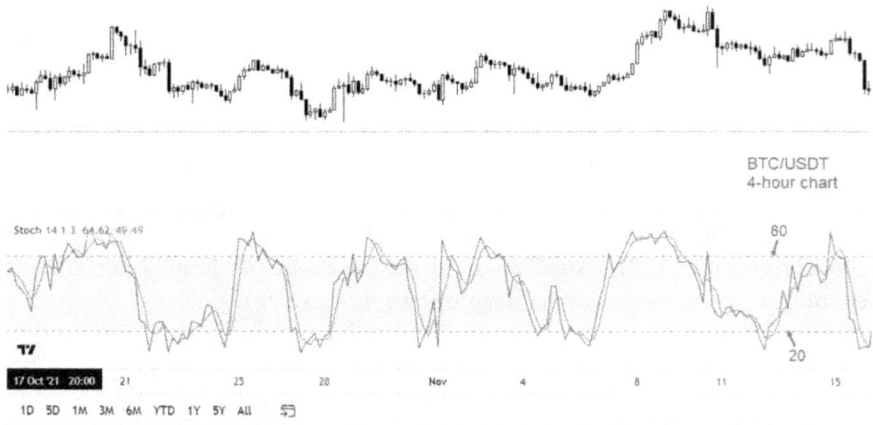

Notice that you can adjust the upper band and lower band values if you want. This can be done with some simple steps below (For me, I hardly change these values).

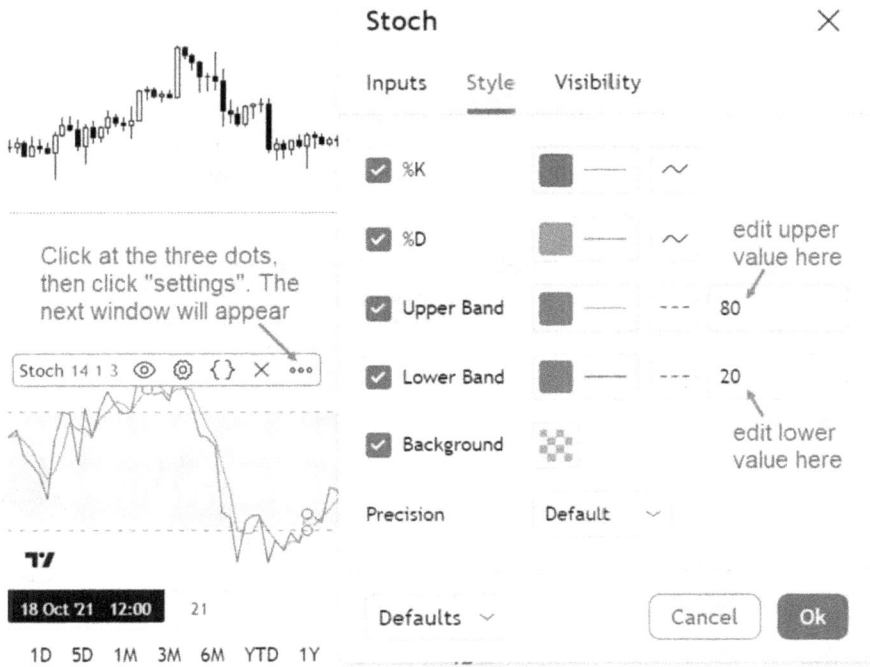

Stoch   ✕

Inputs   Style   Visibility

☑ %K   ⬛ ──── ∿

☑ %D   ⬜ ──── ∿   edit upper value here

☑ Upper Band   ⬛ ──── - - - 80

☑ Lower Band   ⬛ ──── - - - 20

☑ Background   ▨   edit lower value here

Precision   Default ⌄

Defaults ⌄   Cancel   Ok

Click at the three dots, then click "settings". The next window will appear

Stoch 14 1 3 ◎ ⚙ { } ✕ •••

18 Oct '21 12:00   21

1D 5D 1M 3M 6M YTD 1Y

Notes: I am using tradingview.com for presenting trade ideas as well as visual illustrations of technical indicators on the trading chart. Tradingview.com is one of the most popular online trading platforms available. With only a free account, you can get several benefits from the platform.

Also, we will learn different technical indicators in this book. To make it short and simple, whenever you need to change any indicator's input value, locate the "three dots" to the bottom left of the trading chart, then click "setting", and you will open a new window where you can change any input you want.

Keep in mind that the oversold and the overbought areas are for reference only. It's when trade opportunities may appear, but it's not guaranteed in any way.

One common mistake many inexperienced traders may make is to enter a trade just because the price reaches the overbought or oversold zone. This is a good strategy if you want to blow your account away. The market strength driven by the bulls or bears can affect the stochastic reading drastically. In a strong uptrend, the readings can be over 80 for an extended period, causing those who blindly enter short positions to suffer great losses. The same also applies to a sharp downtrend where the price can stay under the 20 level longer than normal.

Now that we have learned that it's not advisable to use any indicator individually, let's see how a trend line and a stochastic oscillator can be combined to determine a trade entry.

In this Litecoin/Tether USD (LTC/USDT) 4-hour chart, we can easily identify a nice uptrend, hence we draw a trend line connecting the lows. Notice how as many lows as possible are connected, resulting in some overlaps while some candlesticks are just about to touch the trend line. As I stated earlier, this is perfectly acceptable in trading.

Look at the highest low in the chart. As the price hits the trend line, there is a possibility of a trend continuation pattern. Meanwhile, the stochastic reading is hovering around the oversold area. This is when we would need to look closer at the two stochastic oscillators.

When there is an intersection between the two stochastic oscillators, it signals a clearer uptrend possibility. We place a long position at the close of the (bullish) candlestick as shown in the picture. Here is what happened next:

LTC/USDT
4-hour chart

entry price

The Litecoin price made a staggering rocket from $197 to $290 in just three days. How crazy it was!

Again, look at how the stochastic reading reacted during the crazy rally. As we see, the reading is well beyond the 80 level. Yet, if a trader blindly entered a short position, he/she might easily endure a (big) loss.

Let's look at another example in a downtrend.

LTC/USDT
4-hour chart

two oscillators cross

trade
entry

Still on Litecoin, in this chart, we spot a clear downtrend, so we connect the highs of the trend. Whenever the price hits the trend line, the stochastic oscillator is overbought.

Let's look at the third trend line touch in the picture. We won't enter any trade until receiving a confirmation signal from the stochastic oscillator – a cross between the two oscillators. Once the intersection occurs, we have the needed signal, and a trade could be placed at the close of the corresponding candlestick (ideally a strong bearish candlestick). Let's see what happened next:

LTC/USDT
4-hour chart

The price fell from $176 to $114 in only one week, a 35% reduction in value.

So, in this section, we've introduced two confirmation triggers that can be combined with trend lines to identify a better win-rate trade entry. Using confirmation signals plays an important part in filtering the unexpected false signals in the market. Moreover, trading on confirmation signals teaches you to be patient in detecting the very best opportunities in the market.

There are not many guarantees I can make to you in financial trading. One thing I can guarantee is that there will be many more opportunities out there. Bear in mind that the crypto market works 24/7, hence opportunities arise regularly. If you cannot find an opportunity now, there will be others soon.

The most ideal timeframe to trade: four-hour chart and longer timeframes (for day trader, swing traders, and long-term investors).

Note: Like some other technical indicators, stochastic oscillators should not be used rigidly. In some cases, you will see the oscillators reverse back before it reaches the overbought or oversold area. For example, an intersection between the two oscillators around the 30 level or even 50 level may also be worth trying a long entry if you get other valued confirmations from a trend line, a support/resistance level, or other types of signals.

In the next section, I will present the specifics of breakout trading – the method I use most often cryptocurrency trading. Also, I will tell you why I am a big fan of a breakout when it comes to cryptocurrency trading.

Breakout Trading

Like pullback trading, breakout trading is also considered a continuation trading method.

We mentioned this trading concept in the previous chapter, and you should get familiar with it. Breakout refers to the price breaking above a resistance level or below a support level, opening the doors for traders to trade in the direction of the breakout candlestick.

Before the breakout happens, the price has normally been kept within a range for some time. This range can be formed by only one trend line which keeps the price under or above it for a period, or two trend lines acting as floor and ceiling where the price tends to bounce back after hitting.

Note: In most examples in this section, the range would be formed by one trend line. Yet, I still introduce some popular double-lined formed patterns so that you have a better idea of how the strategy works in general.

A breakout signals that one side has gained an advantage in pushing the price in their desired direction.

A valid breakout is often accompanied by a high trading volume, which indicates either the bulls or the bears are succeeding in driving the price to their intention. In case the volume connected with the breakout is low, chances are that the breakout can be a fake breakout (or fake-out), and the price may come back to the previous consolidation range. It's not guaranteed to be that, but we should be careful in these cases.

Breakouts are sometimes associated with some patterns such as triangles, rectangles, flags, wedges, etc. These patterns are the results of price movements over a certain period that finally forms recognizable shapes. In the next section, I will introduce some common breakout patterns that could give you an idea of which direction of the trade we should follow.

Triangles

• Ascending triangle

As its name implies, this pattern is often found in an uptrend when the price encounters a strong (horizontal) resistance and a series of higher lows is created as the price tries to poke through the resistance level.

An ascending triangle can tell you two things. First, the buyers are having difficulties in breaking the resistance level/area. Second, the seller's pressure is weaker and weaker, resulting in higher lows and indicating the bears are more likely to lose the battle in the near future.

- Descending triangle

The descending triangle is opposite to an ascending triangle, normally occurring during a downtrend. This is characterized by a (horizontal) support level and a series of lower highs. In this condition, the price movements are rejected by the support area multiple times, but the buying momentum diminishes within the same period, forming more bearish candlesticks and less bullish ones within the range. This is a typical bearish continuation pattern.

- Symmetrical triangle

A symmetrical triangle is a continuation pattern and can be found in both uptrend and downtrend.

Lower highs

Higher lows

A symmetrical pattern is characterized by higher lows and lower highs, which look like a squeeze. This suggests that neither the bulls nor the bears have more advantage in the market.

In a typical symmetrical pattern, the price is likely to break the triangle in the direction of the dominant trend. For example, if the dominant trend is up, then a breakout is likely to occur at the resistance of the triangle, attracting more long positions.

Due to its shape, a symmetrical pattern is also known as a pennant. A typical pennant neither slopes upward nor downward.

Traders who favor pennants trading might choose to either trade on the close of the breakout candlestick or place a trade on a pullback at the trend line. It may seem confusing, but don't worry. Later in this book, I'll describe in detail which method I use and the reason behind it

Wedge patterns

Like pennant patterns, there are two different forms of wedge patterns, including bullish and bearish formation. As their names say, these patterns look like a wedge. Let's look at some examples below:

Downtrend

Price breaks and continues with trend

Price breaks and continues with trend

Uptrend

Unlike pennants, wedge patterns are either upward or downward. While this can be used in both reversal and continuation trading, I prefer using it in a trend continuation. Moreover, a wedge pattern slope is steeper than the horizontal support/resistance level, and its price movement range gets smaller and smaller over time before a breakout happens.

Flag pattern

Similar to a wedge pattern, a flag pattern's slope is steeper than the horizontal support/resistance level. However, the price range remains unchanged in width during the consolidation period before a breakout happens and the trend continues.

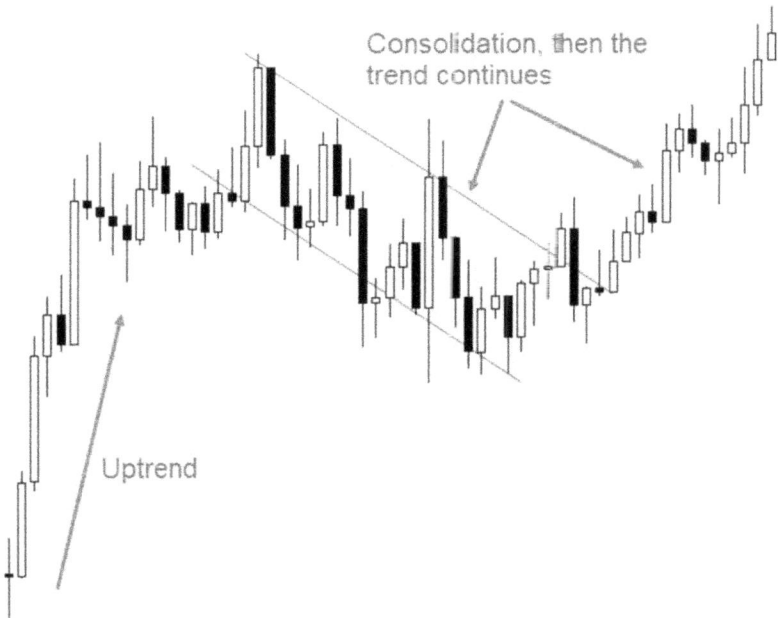

In this bullish flag pattern, the price is angled lower during the consolidation. In some cases, it could also be directly sideways within a rectangle shape. A lower angled range like this indicates the bears are in control of the battle short term before the bulls jump in.

Downtrend

Consolidation, then the trend continues

In this bearish flag pattern, the consolidation range also has an angled slope to the upside, meaning that the buyers are gaining strength short term. The bears are losing steam during this period and cannot take control of the battle until later.

Now that you have a general picture of what the breakout patterns are and how they are categorized into different types, let's take a deeper look to see why it happens in the financial market. Consider the picture below:

ETH/USDT
4-hour chart

a breakout

3587.58
3450.00
3330.00
3210.00
3090.00
2990.00
2890.00
2790.00
2710.00

This is a rectangle pattern where the price continuously bounces back upon hitting support and resistance levels, indicating that neither buyers nor sellers have an advantage during the consolidation period. When a breakout happens, for example, to the upside of the range, the buyers are in control of the battle. When buyers are becoming stronger, sellers are forced to close their position around the resistance level (i.e just above the support level – where most of the stop-losses are placed).

As the sellers are stopped out and buyers keep gaining more strength, a continuation of the upside is inevitable, not to mention many other traders are initiating their long positions as well after spotting a nice opportunity in the market.

All these (psychological) factors directly affect the price movements (often sharp ones) after a successful breakout is confirmed. As I mentioned above, a valid breakout is often supported by accelerating trading volume.

Trading breakouts has always been my favorite method. In the following sections, I will reveal some simple and effective techniques to identify reliable breakouts and initiate a trade. Those are the ones I have been using for years.

Strategy No.1: Momentum candlestick

The first technique I want to reveal in this chapter is connected with momentum candlesticks.

In the previous section, you learned about many types of breakout patterns. One question may arise: Do I need to remember all the characteristics of each pattern?

The answer is "Yes" and "No".

It should be "Yes" because it helps you identify each price pattern easily. However, I rarely remember each of the patterns myself, but still make good use of these patterns. Why is that?

If you notice, each breakout pattern is formed from two frontiers: the upper line and the lower line, representing resistance and support respectively. The range between the upper limit and the lower limit is the consolidation area, and it's where we wait for a breakout to happen. Put differently, identifying support and resistance successfully will eventually result in one of the five breakout patterns mentioned above.

Doing this, you will not have to remember each characteristic of each pattern individually because support and resistance have done the heavy lifting for you. What you need to remember, instead, is the four attributes in drawing support and resistance levels that I discussed in the previous chapter.

This is why I always emphasize the importance of support & resistance in trading any type of asset.

While the breakout patterns are often connected with the continuation of the trend, there are cases where they signal a price reversal instead. Hence, an effective breakout trading strategy entails a reliable method of defining the direction of the breakout.

A common mistake that inexperienced traders often make is that they enter a position right after the breakout candlestick. Let's take a look at the Luna chart below:

LUNA/USDT
daily chart

slight break

0.38
0.36
0.34
0.33
0.32
0.31
0.30
0.29
0.29
0.28
0.27

14   Oct   19   Nov

As you can see, the consolidation area is a rectangle pattern, which is formed between two parallel horizontal lines. After multiple touches at both support and resistance, the price slightly broke below the support level. If you have no idea about a momentum candlestick, you might blindly enter a short position, with might cause a loss as shown in the picture below:

LUNA/USDT
daily chart

price rockets after
the fake-out

breakout becomes fake-out

As you can see, just the appearance of a breakout does not guarantee successive moves in the direction of the breakout candlestick. In a highly volatile market like cryptocurrency, there is often a risk of a false breakout, where the price rapidly comes back to the consolidation zone and sweeps your stop loss.

This is where a momentum candlestick may help you. A momentum candlestick can be found in a marubozu with a very long body with little or no wick or shadow. Also, it can be a collection of some consecutive medium-sized candlesticks pushing through the support/resistance levels without any difficulties.

A momentum candlestick can give a better chance of a successful break. This is when the breakout side has gained enough strength to drive the price to its expected level while the opposing side has become weaker and unable to remain active.

To gain a better understanding of the efficiency of a momentum candlestick, have a look at another example.

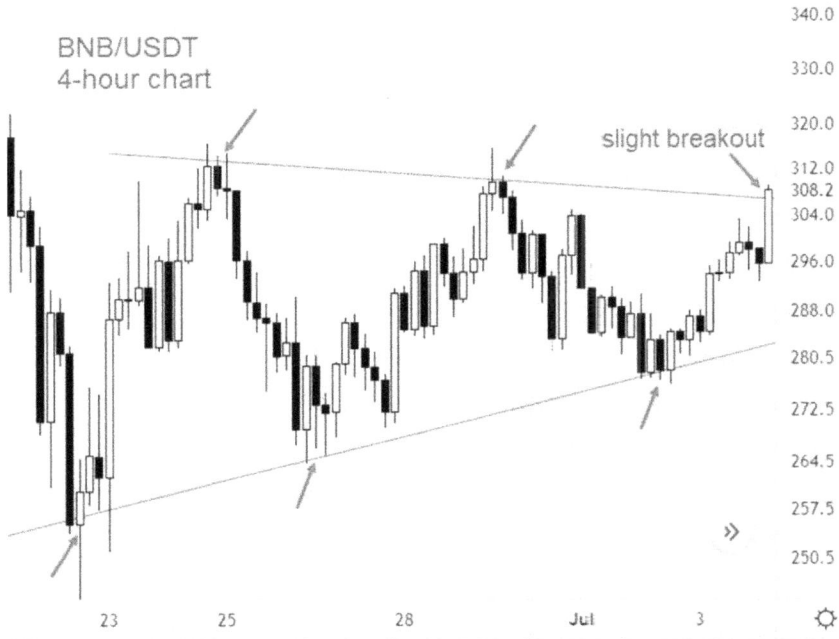

BNB/USDT
4-hour chart

slight breakout

This is the Binance price chart in late June and early July 2021. We can easily define lower highs and higher lows in the chart. Hence, it somewhat resembles a pennant, though the lower frontier seems to be steeper than the higher one. After a few hits at both support and resistance, the price finally broke above the resistance level. However, by looking closely at the breakout, most of the candlestick's body is inside the consolidation range. Hence, this candlestick is not treated as an indicator of momentum, although it is a marubozu per definition.

In a situation like this, it is advisable to wait for the close of the next candlestick(s) to see whether the bulls are actually in control of the price.

Unfortunately, the next few candlesticks don't show any clear direction of an uptrend, so we should sit on the sideline in this situation.

After a few more candlesticks, a momentum candlestick formed.

Unlike the previous one, this marubozu is the momentum candlestick we are looking for. Notice how the total body of this candlestick breaks outside the resistance level, forming a longer candlestick than most of the previous ones. An entry order can be placed at the close of a momentum candlestick and a stop-loss below the higher limit of the triangle.

If you have experience trading other types of assets, or if you have read some other book about trend line trading, you may ask me why I don't wait for a retest before placing an order.

For some of you who haven't heard about "retest", it indicates the price coming back to the old support/resistance level before continuing its way. Take a look at the example below:

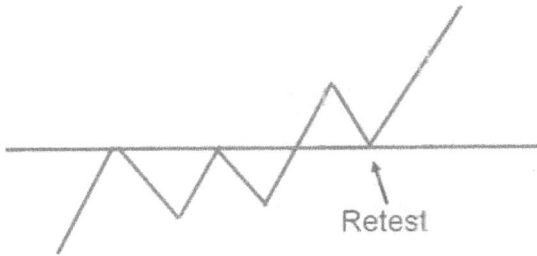

Retest

A lot of traders (including professional ones) love trading on a retest. The idea behind that is the price often "remembers" the old key level, where resistance can turn into support, and vice versa. I am also a fan of trading on a retest, but not always. In the market with sharp and quick moves like crypto, trading without a retest fascinates me more. Here is the logic behind placing an entry at the close of the breakout (momentum) candlestick.

Let's consider three possible scenarios and weigh their pros and cons.

Scenario 1: From the breakout candlestick, the price shoots up immediately: we would stack a nice profit. This is the best scenario.

Scenario 2: From the breakout candlestick, the price retests the resistance level before rising: This is called pullback trading, or trading on a retest, which I mentioned above. In this case, we still have a chance of making a nice profit, although it may take longer (since the stop-loss is placed below the prior resistance level).

Scenario 3: From the breakout candlestick, the price deeply reversed into the consolidation area again. In this case, we suffer a loss. Yet, from my experience, the possibility of this happening is lower than the other two options. Remember we base our decision on a momentum candlestick which can act as a directional one. Even if suffer a loss in this case, by setting a stop loss below the resistance, the loss amount is completely under control, and we can accept it.

On the other hand, if we always wait for a retest, we can miss many good trade opportunities where the price makes sharp moves toward the direction of the breakout. The profits we miss can be (much) bigger than the losses we may encounter on trading without a retest.

Again, this is not about being right or wrong. It is my preferred method of entering a trade based on a momentum candlestick. If you are a more conservative trader and trading on a retest makes you more comfortable, just stick to it and measure its effectiveness.

Strategy No. 2: Momentum loss

The second confirmation signal we'll discuss in this chapter is a loss of momentum.

We've learned about a loss of momentum in the previous chapter, with candlesticks becoming smaller and smaller as they approach the support/resistance level.

The loss of momentum we'll address in this section covers a bigger range in the market, where the entry price level is determined based on the price momentum in close connection with the use of the trend line. Let's look at the picture below:

In this 4-hour Litecoin chart, the price is making a smooth downtrend, hence a trend line is drawn by connecting the highs. You can see that the market was continuously forming lower lows for most of the period. However, when looking at the latest price action, it fails to create a lower low. This indicates the bears are losing their steam and a possible trend reversal may occur. This reversal can be further confirmed by the directional candlestick pattern – a long bullish candlestick that breaks the trend line. A trade entry can be placed at the close of the candlestick, with the stop-loss placed below the breakout candle.

Here is what happened later following the breakout.

The trend reversed strongly from the breakout candlestick. By listening to what the market tells via price action patterns, trading breakouts become less risky and more effective.

Now, take a look at another example:

BTC/USDT
1-hour chart

momentum loss

67000.00
66000.00
65200.00
64400.00
63600.00
62737.67
62050.00
61250.00
60450.00
59650.00
58950.00
58230.00

breakout but not a
directional candlestick

entry price at the close
of this candlestick

18   19   20   21

This is the BTC/USDT 1-hour chart. There is a clear uptrend in place, hence we connect the lows on the chart to form a trend line below the candlesticks. Again, notice how the bulls are dominating the game for a long time until they start to lose their bullish momentum at the end of the rally. This is defined by a lower high at just above the $66,000 price level. It's the first sign of an imminent trend reversal.

From this high, the price breaks the trend line to the downside. Yet, it is not a strong bearish candlestick, illustrated by long shadows at both ends of the candlestick. Because of this, it's advisable to look for a more reliable bearish pattern on the chart.

After some time, we found another bearish candlestick, with its body longer than most of the previous ones. Entering a short entry at the close of this candle would be a good decision. Let's look at what happened next:

BTC/USDT
1-hour chart

entry price

67000.00
66000.00
65200.00
64400.00
63600.00
62800.00
62050.00
61250.00
60450.00
59859.97
58950.00

21   22   23   24

The price shows certain indecision at first. However, over time, the downtrend outshined and the bears would reap a nice profit.

Another popular candlestick pattern that indicates a loss of momentum is the double top/bottom. Take a look at the example below:

XRP/USDT
1-hour chart

entry at the close
of the breakout
candlestick

1.1400
1.1200
1.1000
1.0850
1.0700
1.0550
1.0430
1.0310
1.0190

14   15   16

In this Ripple/Tether USD (XRP/USDT) chart, the price is constantly making higher highs until the latest one, which fails to reach a higher price level. This indicates a loss in the upside momentum and is the first sign of a potential trend reversal.

However, we should not opt for a short position until receiving additional confirmation from the market. A momentum breaking down below the trend line may be a good trigger that we need. As it turns out in the picture below, entering a trade at the close of the breakout candlestick can be a wise decision.

Below is an example about a double bottom pattern:

580.0
569.2
57:00
~~560.0~~
540.0

directional
candlestick

525.0
513.0
503.2

488.5
478.5

BCH/USDT
4-hour chart

double bottom

468.5
458.5

22   24   12:00   27   29   Oc ☼

This is the Bitcoin Cash/Tether USD (BCH/USDT) 4-hour chart in late September 2021. The market was in a strong downtrend until a double bottom shaped, indicating a loss of downward momentum on the chart. From the bottom, the price broke above the trend line, yet the breakout candlestick was not strong enough for confirming a long entry.

It is the next candlestick (a marubozu) that indicates a direction. This candle has a longer body than most of the previous ones, and a very short shadow, indicating strong bullish momentum. Initiating a trade at the close of this candlestick would be a good decision. Below is what happened next:

BCH/USDT
4-hour chart

Entry price

620.0
613.1
600.0
580.0
566.9
44:16
545.0
530.0
518.0
506.0
493.5
483.5
473.5
463.5

29   Oct   12:00   4   6

The price rose from $500 to $625 (a 25% rise in value) in just one week. It would be a very nice trade with an ideal risk/reward ratio.

Exit price:

There are many ways to look for an appropriate target price. As I mentioned, support/resistance is what I consider the priority on choosing an exit price. Moreover, you can use the techniques mentioned in the previous chapter regarding the loss of momentum in candlesticks to consider closing a trade.

In Chapter 12, I will reveal some different methods of exiting a trade after you have identified the target price. This will help you be more flexible and effective in closing your trades under various circumstances, better coping with market fluctuations.

Why are breakouts suitable for cryptocurrency trading?

We have all known a breakout can initiate a strong momentum afterward, hence it can be ideal for trading assets with a big movement magnitude. As can be seen through many trade examples up to now, the cryptocurrency market is famous for its crazy price movements within a short period. For example, at the time of this writing (2021), it's normal for a crypto price to change around 20-30 percent within just a few days. This is the main reason why breakout trading is suitable for cryptocurrencies.

Among many strategies I implement in crypto trading, breakout trading has been the most used method by far in determining trade entries and stop-losses.

Ideal Timeframes:

Breakout trading can be effective in day trading (one-hour, four-hour, daily charts), swing trading (4-hour, daily, weekly, monthly charts), and long-term trading.

I am not a fan of scalping, so it's hard for me to tell whether it can work well on a one-minute or five-minute chart. If you are a newbie, it is better to stay away from this type of trading. Period!

Note: The methods presented in this chapter should be treated like ones that give you better trade options instead of guaranteeing any trading success. No method could give you a guarantee of success. Trading is all about probability. Yet, if you constantly focus on optimizing every trade you are in, you will stand a higher chance of winning. When your winning trades consistently outshine your losing ones, you will be winning overall. This is called consistently profitable.

Key Takeaways:

- Analyze price actions carefully at a key level (ideally with at least one more method);

- Momentum candlestick is highly recommended in entering a trade;

- Be flexible in using momentum analysis in trading;

In short, breakout trading is, without question, the simplest and the most effective trading method that I've ever used. Yet, it is risky to apply unless you exert certain reliable techniques in avoiding false signals and identifying good opportunities.

In the next chapter, I will describe one more way of trading breakout using confirmation from a technical indicator.

Chapter 8: Relative Strength Index

Being mainly a price action trader, I prefer reading candlestick patterns than trading purely on signals from any technical indicator. However, this does not mean I refute the role of indicators in cryptc trading.

You have learned about support/resistance and trend lines as the core of an effective trading system in previous chapters. In this chapter, I will talk about an indicator that acts more like a reliable confirmation signal which greatly helps you in making your trading decisions.

What is the RSI?

RSI is the abbreviation of Relative Strength Index, measuring the magnitude of recent price changes to determine the oversold and overbought areas in the price of an asset. The RSI is determined based on price fluctuations during a certain period (default value is 14). Normally, you don't need to change this default value.

The RSI is displayed as an oscillator whose reading ranges between two extremes (zero and one hundred). As a default, any reading of 70 or above is overbought while the reading of 30 or below indicates oversold. Moreover, when the index surpasses the 30 level, this may be treated as a bullish signal, meanwhile, a slide below the 70 level can be considered a bearish sign.

During an extended uptrend, the price may remain in the overbought zone longer than usual. A similar result can also happen in a strong downtrend where the price may remain in the oversold area longer than expected.

From another angle, in an uptrend, the RSI reading mostly reaches the 70 level and rarely hovers around the 30 level. Whereas, in a downtrend, the reading would frequently hit the oversold area and rarely violate the overbought zone.

A common mistake in trading RSI

One common mistake that a lot of traders make when using RSI is they place a long position when the reading is oversold and initiate a short position when the index reaches the overbought area. This is a good trading method… if you want to throw your money away.

The RSI may release some "false" signals many times. This is especially true if the trend is very strong, which I mentioned above. In these situations, the reading may hover around the overbought or oversold area longer than usual.

Here is an example of this.

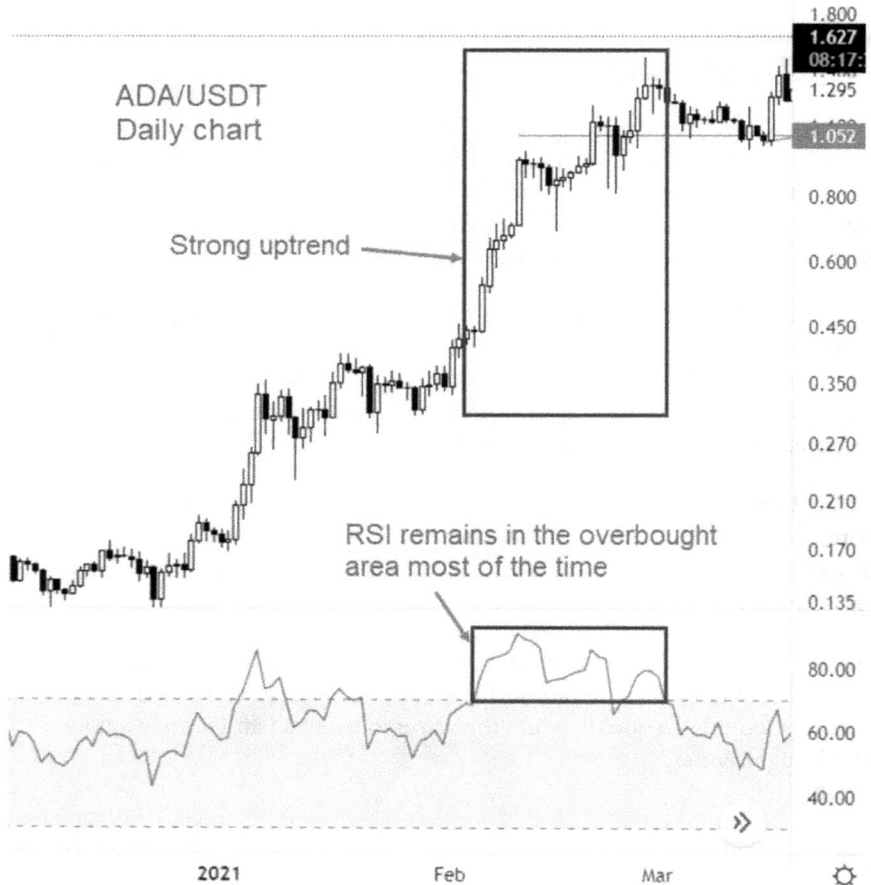

This is the daily Cardano/Tether USD (ADA/USDT) chart from early 2021. As you can see, the Cardano price made a crazy surge – tenfold in just three months. In this period, February is when the market saw the most substantial increase in price. However, when looking at the RSI reading, it remained solidly in the overbought area in the same period. If any trader chose to place a short position in February based on the overbought zone, it's very likely that he/she would end up in a loss.

In short, just because the RSI hit the oversold or overbought area does not mean that a reversal will occur. As I mentioned, instead of relying on the RSI as the main indicator in your trading system, we should use it as the supporting signal to further confirm a trade setup or a trigger. Let's break this into different techniques in the next section so that you can have a better understanding of how it works. But first, let's discover how to display RSI on the chart on tradingview.com.

Let's look at some simple steps below:

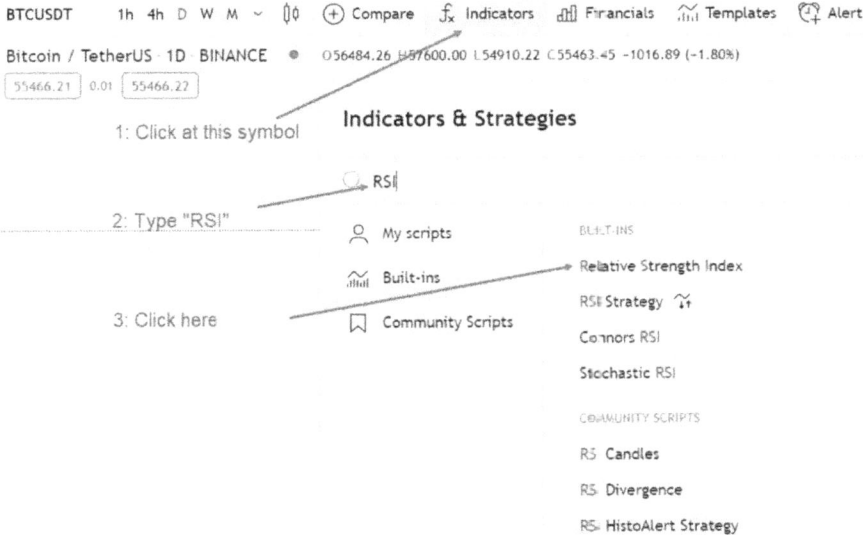

While there are some other RSI trading methods, in this chapter, I only introduce three methods that I think may offer higher chances of winning. Let's address them below:

Strategy 1: RSI Regular Divergences

You may have heard about the Regular Divergences before, but we'll briefly introduce the concept here so you can have a better understanding of what it is and when it happens.

First, RSI regular divergence is the sign of a potential reversal, which is categorized into two types: a bullish divergence and a bearish divergence.

A bullish divergence occurs when the price is making lower lows while the RSI indicator is making higher lows. Technically speaking, the failure to form a lower low indicates the downward momentum is becoming weaker and weaker, signaling a reversal from a downtrend to an uptrend. The image below illustrates this pattern:

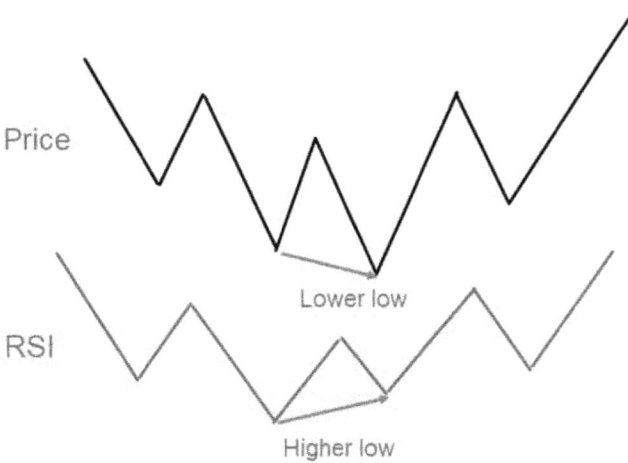

Meanwhile, a bearish divergence appears when the market is making higher highs but the RSI is making lower highs at the same time. This may signal that the previous dominant side is losing its steam in pushing the market toward a higher high, and the bears may take control in a near future. The below picture illustrates how a bearish convergence looks:

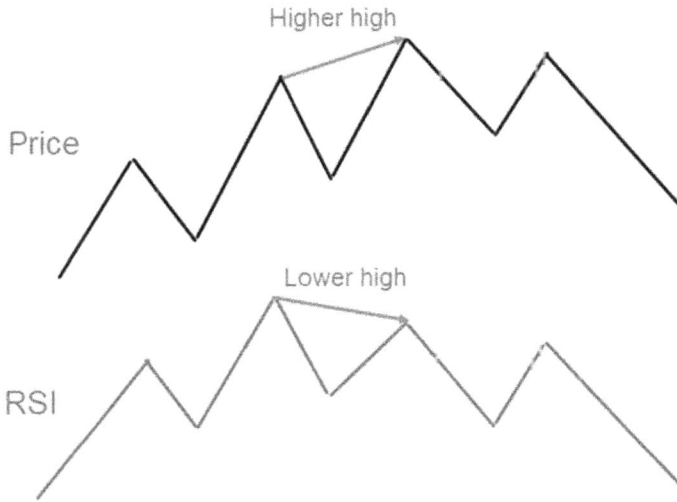

Higher high

Price

Lower high

RSI

In short, the RSI regular divergence occurs when the RSI moves in a different direction to the price, signaling that the momentum is starting to shift and the previous trend won't be sustained.

Once again, I must emphasize that placing a trade just because an RSI divergence appears could lead to a disastrous outcome. Sometimes, the RSI divergence alone can release false signals. Hence, it's a must that you obtain another entry signal from at least one more trading tool. Being a big fan of trading with support/resistance, let me show you how to combine them with an RSI convergence to open a position.

Principle:

Combine the regular RSI divergence with a trend line and a directional candlestick to look for a trade setup and trigger.

Take a look at the example below:

BTC/USDT
1-hour chart

directional candlestick

RSI divergence

This is the (Bitcoin/Tether USD) BTC/USDT chart in September 2021. As you can see, the pair was in an uptrend and a trend line could be drawn to connect the lows on the chart. The trend line serves as a support line that rejects the price multiple times along the trend.

Toward the end of the trend line, a bullish divergence appears when the price continues to form a higher high while the corresponding RSI reading shows a slight downward momentum. This divergence signals a potential price drop soon. However, we won't place a trade until we receive a reliable confirmation signal.

To confirm a reversal, we should prudently wait for the price to break the trend line successfully with a directional (momentum) candlestick. In this example, the breakout candlestick is a marubozu which signals the bears are active and ready to dominate the market. An entry could be placed at the close of the bearish candlestick.

As you can see in the chart below, the price plummeted after the appearance of the momentum candlestick.

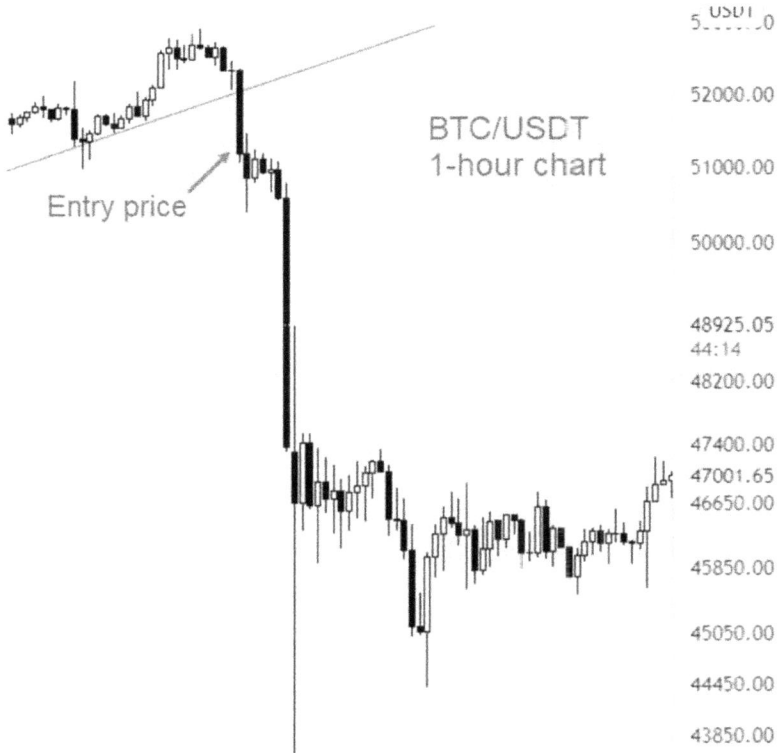

BTC/USDT
1-hour chart

Entry price

Let's look at another example on the Bitcoin 1-hour chart:

breakout candlestick

BTC/USDT
1-hour chart

Bullish convergence

In this chart, the market is in a nice uptrend, and we draw a trend line to connect some swing highs on the chart. Toward the end of the uptrend, we can easily identify a bearish divergence formed by the downward direction of the price matched with correspondingly higher lows in the RSI reading. This may be the signal for a reversal from an uptrend to a downtrend.

Next, we wait for a breakout to the upside of the trend line, ideally with a momentum candlestick. Notice that in this case, the breakout candlestick does not indicate momentum because of its medium-sized body.

Remember that this can happen frequently in the financial market, where we just miss the last condition for a trade to trigger. The market doesn't always provide some approval signals at the same time, and trading is not black and white.

Have a look at the chart below.

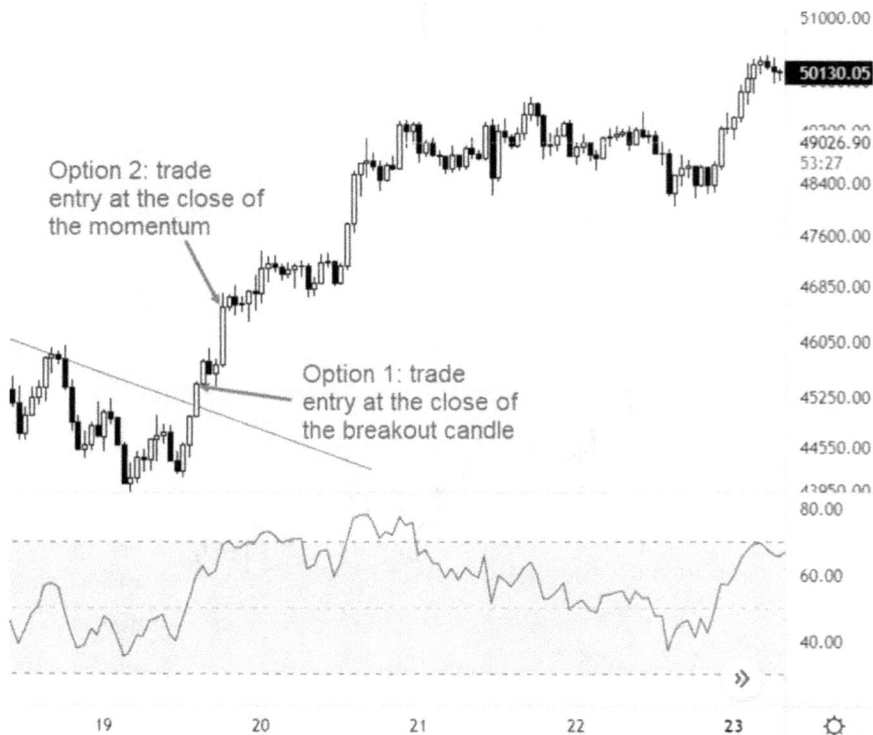

The market advances nicely from the breakout. You can place a trade (1) at the close of the breakout candle or (2) at the close of the momentum candlestick (with a longer body and a clearer directional function). Trading with a momentum candlestick helps us filter out many false signals in the market.

Also, the latter wouldn't earn you many profits in this case.

This is a simple but effective trading technique using a combination of RSI regular divergence, a trend line, and a momentum candlestick, which helps to better stack the odds in your favor. In the next section, you will learn about another type of RSI divergence - the hidden divergence.

Strategy 2: RSI Hidden Divergence

Looking at the name of the tool, you may wonder whether this type of divergence is harder to spot in the market. Don't worry, it is just how it is named, and identifying it would not be difficult after you read this section.

Similar to a regular divergence, hidden divergence can be categorized into bullish patterns and bearish patterns. However, unlike a regular divergence, a hidden divergence indicates a potential trend continuation. Let's dig deeper into this.

Bullish Hidden Divergence

A hidden bullish divergence occurs when the price is forming higher lows and the RSI is forming lower lows within the same period. You can spot this type of divergence during a consolidation phase after a nice uptrend, in which the price may continue its upward movements even though the RSI is heading downward. This suggests that the overall trend is still bullish and the consolidation may be the result of the profit-taking among buyers rather than the emergence of a reversal. In other words, the uptrend can be expected to resume.

Take a look at the example below:

ETH/USDT
4-hour chart

strong marubozu

higher low

lower low

3600.00
3414.22
3250.00
3090.00
2965.00
2845.00
2735.00
80.00
60.00
40.00
20.00

Oct   4   7

In this Ethereum/Tether USD (ETH/USDT) 4-hour chart, you can see after a nice uptrend, the market sees a pullback with a strong bearish marubozu. While you may think that this candlestick can be dangerous for the bulls, the RSI tells it differently. Specifically, the marubozu matches a correspondingly lower low in the RSI reading, indicating that the uptrend may continue. Here is what happened later.

ETH/USDT
4-hour chart

Strong uptrend continued

The uptrend resumed successfully after a pullback, and the RSI divergence predicted the trend continuation correctly.

Bearish Hidden Divergence

Conversely, a bearish hidden divergence occurs when the price is forming a lower high while the RSI is forming a higher high during the same period. This pattern can be identified in a downtrend, indicating that the sellers are taking a rest before continuing the downtrend. Put differently, the sellers are still taking control of the battle and the consolidation is likely to be short-lived before the downtrend continues. Take a look at an Ethereum 1-hour chart:

In this example, a downtrend is in place for the first half of the chart. During this period, the RSI is also heading downward. Then, the bulls jumped in and pushed the price to the upside. This is when a bearish hidden divergence is confirmed because the price makes a lower high while the RSI forms a higher high. This indicates a possibility that the downtrend may resume. As you can see in the picture below, the RSI once again predicts the trend continuation correctly.

A trap on trading with RSI divergence

In real trading, detecting a correct hidden divergence may not be as easy as presented above. In the two examples above, the most important element to look for is the end of a correction. It is when the RSI divergence is confirmed and traders should watch out for a trade entry soon.

You must be confident that what you are looking for is a correction of the trend. It is often time-consuming or even disastrous if you mistake an impulse for a correction.

To avoid this mistake, you must identify which type of divergence you are looking for, a bullish one or a bearish one?

If the overall trend is bullish, you only look for a correction in an uptrend. Otherwise, if the dominant trend is bearish, a correction of a downtrend is what you should expect. Yet, whether the trend is bullish or bearish depends on which timeframe you are trading. For example, the market can be bullish on a daily chart, but be bearish on a 1-hour chart.

One indicator I often use in identifying a reliable overall trend in the market is the Exponential Moving Average (EMA).

EMA is calculated by dividing the sum of the closing price during a certain number of periods by that period in the observation. Accordingly, the 200 EMA is the result of a sum of the latest 200 closing prices divided by 200. The 200 EMA is considered the most widely used indicator for determining the long-term trend. When the price of an asset crosses the 200 EMA from below, it is the signal that the bulls are still dominating the market, and vice versa.

When trading with RSI divergence, the principle in using EMA is simple: If the price is above the 200 EMA, you should look for a bullish divergence, and if the price is below the 200 EMA, you should only look for a bearish divergence.

Trading RSI hidden divergence

While the RSI hidden divergence can be used in different ways, let's discover how to combine it with a stochastic oscillator to identify a trade entry.

The principle is simple: When you have successfully determined a hidden RSI divergence, wait for the two oscillators to cross and a directional candlestick to form before identifying a trade entry.

As you learned in the previous chapter, this oscillator helps determine the overbought and oversold areas in the chart as well as the transformation of the market power shown by the intersection between the two lines.

Now, let's move to an example:

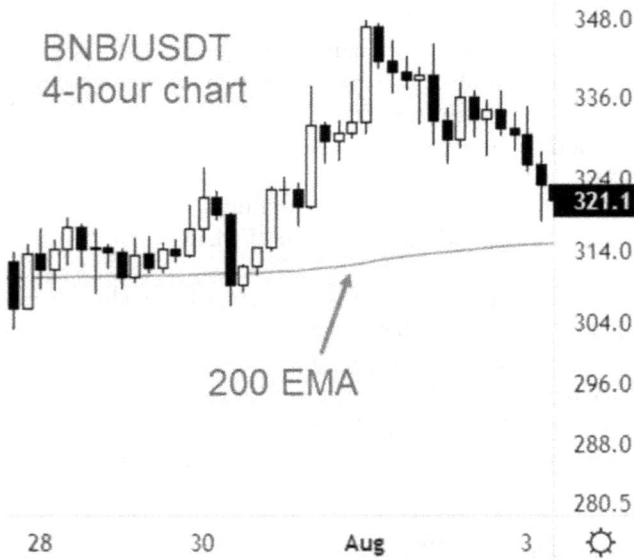

BNB/USDT
4-hour chart

200 EMA

348.0
336.0
324.0
321.1
314.0
304.0
296.0
288.0
280.5

28   30   Aug   3

This is the Binance/Tether USD (BNB/USDT) 4-hour chart in late July and early August 2021. In this example, the current price was above the 200 EMA line. Hence, we only look for a long position. Now, let's employ RSI and stochastic oscillator to see what happened:

BNB/USDT
4-hour chart

higher low

lower low

oscillator at oversold area

350.0
340.0
328.0
323.3
320.0
310.0
302.0
294.0

60.00
40.00
20.00

80.00
40.00
0.00

29   Aug

168

As we can see, the price was temporarily forming a higher low while the RSI was forming a lower low. I use the word "temporary" because the market still moves and we cannot conclude that this is the final "end of correction" at this time.

In trading, you would watch out for divergence in a case like this because it may happen. Also, notice the corresponding stochastic oscillator was oversold, which is the reason we need to focus on the next price action even more. Let's see what happened next:

Look at how the market formed several indecision candlesticks after following the bearish correction period. Next, the RSI turned out to be upward at the same time, confirming the bullish hidden divergence that we are looking for.

Next, the stochastic oscillators crossed to the upside, meaning the bullish momentum was back again in the market. Hence, we have one more confirmation signal to enter the trade. Yet, this cross corresponded with an indecision candlestick on the chart, which is not very ideal to enter a trade.

To further confirm an entry point, a directional/momentum candlestick whose body is longer than most of the previous candlesticks is recommended. As we can see, it would not take long for that candlestick to form on the chart. An entry could be placed at the close of this candlestick. As you can see in the picture below, the uptrend continued smoothly afterward.

Initiating a trade with the backup of a directional candlestick could save you from many false signals. Moreover, while trading based on a single technical indicator could be dangerous due to market unpredictability, a combination of at least three indicators does increase the probability of a winning trade.

Let's look at another example below in a downtrend.

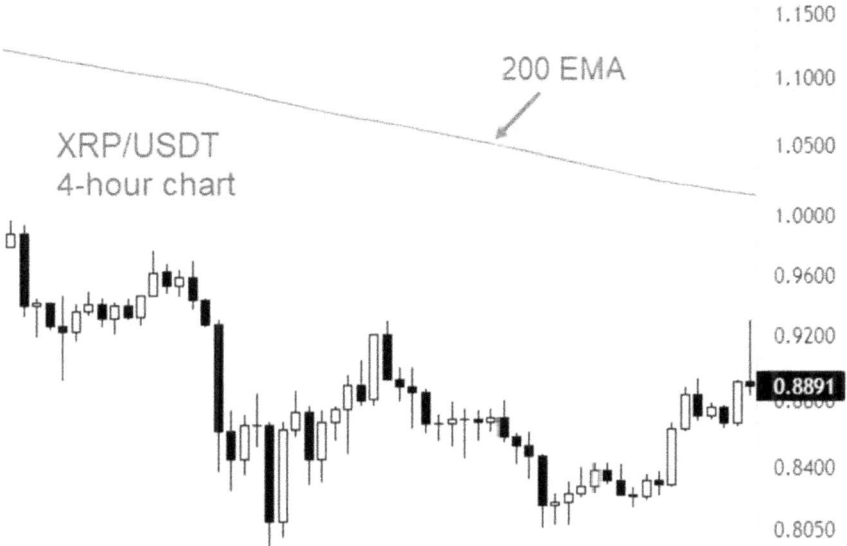

This is the XRP/USDT 4-hour chart, and the price is well below the 200 EMA. This means we should look for a short entry only.

Now, let's equip the chart with the RSI and stochastic oscillator to see what happens.

XRP/USDT
4-hour chart

oscillator at the overbought area

In the first place, the downtrend is characterized by lower highs on the chart. However, from the third high, a lot of indecision candlesticks appear with a very small body, indicating the bears are losing their steam for a while. Toward the end of the chart, some bullish candlesticks form, but we are not able to confirm a complete trend correction yet. Also, the stochastic oscillator is overbought at this point. Let's see what happens next:

directional candle

0.9600

0.9200

0.8891

0.8400

XRP/USDT
4-hour chart

0.7956
03:15:3

60.00

40.00

20.00

wait for oscillators to cross

80.00

40.00

0.00

7   10   14

After a few more candlesticks, we now have the expected RSI hidden divergence, with the market forming a lower high, matching with a higher high in the RSI reading.

Next, notice the stochastic oscillators cross to the downside, indicating the bearish momentum can be back again in the market. We now have one more confirmation to place a short entry.

Lastly, when looking back to the chart, a rejection pin bar forms, with a long tail and a very small body. This further indicates that the downward trend is now in place. An entry could be placed at the close of this candlestick. As you can see in the picture below, the price drops from around $0.9 to as low as $0.5 in around one week.

Keep in mind that the market will not always plummet or skyrocket in the examples above. These are real examples to show you that you can make huge profits sometimes if you are consistent with the trading strategy I am introducing as well as avoiding violating any of the risk management rules.

Another point to note is that you don't even need to make huge profits to be a successful trader. As a trader, being consistently profitable is much more important than doubling your account in a short period. As George Soros says:

"It's not whether you're right or wrong that's important, it's how much money you make when you're right and how much you lose when you're wrong".

Profit-taking and Stop-loss Placement

The profit you make depends on when and how you take profits. Regarding the "how", I will discuss it in more detail in a separate chapter in this book. The question of when to take profits may have different answers. While the idea of exiting trades based on support/resistance and a loss of prevailing momentum will always be my priority, you might consider taking profits based on a fixed risk-reward ratio. In my opinion, the minimum ratio for taking a profit is 1:2, meaning that for every loss that you risk, there is a twofold reward if the market goes favorably.

Exiting based on the fixed risk/reward ratio can be applied when the next support/resistance is quite far away and the market is experiencing a wild volatility period. This exit technique could be applied to both regular divergence and hidden divergence trading.

Again, the market may poke through your profit-taking level and advance or drop much further (depending on whether you go long or go short), but it's part of the game. You should accept it and be happy with your profit. Don't be so greedy and raise your take-profit level further, and further, and further without clearly determining your profit objective.

Regarding the stop loss level, placing the stop order just above the nearest swing high in case of a bearish hidden divergence and just below the swing low in case of a bullish hidden divergence is a safe enough option.

Note: Tradingview.com contains many indicators coded and uploaded by traders. At the time of this writing, there has not been an individually coded 200 EMA indicator for traders. Yet, you can still make use of this indicator by following some simple steps below:

Indicators & Strategies   ✕

ema ━━━━━━ Step 2: Type "ema" in the search bar

☆ Favorites

FAVORITES

☆ Moving Average Exponential

○ My scripts

BUILT-INS

〜 Built-ins

☆ Moving Average Exponential

□ Community Scripts

Double EMA

Triple EMA

COMMUNITY SCRIPTS

EMA Wave Indicator [LazyBear]   LazyBear   7289

EMA 20/50/100/200   drsweets   5825

Step 3: Click at this
result

EMA Enveloper Indicator & a crazy prediction   LazyBear   5065

EMA   DkSwag   4290

Afterward, three exponential moving average lines would appear on the chart: the 20 Day, 50 Day, and 200 Day lines. You'll need to remove the 20 Day and 50 Day lines from your chart. Just follow some simple steps below:

Step 1: left click at one of these lines

⏱ Add Alert on EMA (0.9778)...   Alt + A

〜 Add Indicator/Strategy on EMA ...

◈ Visual Order   >

⇔ Move To   >   Step 2: right click at
                                               one of these lines
↳ Pin To Scale (Now Right)   >

Source Code...

Copy   Ctrl + C

⊘ Hide

🗑 Remove   Del   Step 3: Click at
                                          "settings"

Object Tree...

⚙ Settings...

16   Sep   16   Oct   16   Nov   16   Dec

A new window will appear. Next, just untick the 20 day and 50 day moving average, and you now have only the 200 Exponential Moving Average on your chart.

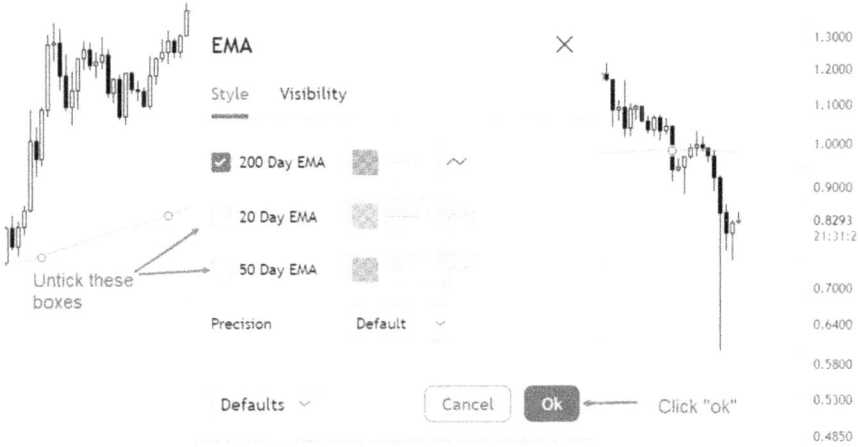

Breakout strategy with RSI indicator

We've learned about breakout trading in combination with the RSI regular divergence in the first section of this chapter. In this section, we'll discover another aspect of RSI in breakout trading.

As I mentioned at the beginning of the chapter, the RSI's surpassing above the 30 level may signal a bullish momentum while a slide below the 70 level may be the indication of a potential downtrend. Yet, for better identification of a trend continuation, I prefer to wait for the RSI to cross the mid-way marker – the 50 RSI level.

The underlying principle is simple: The RSI crossing above the 50 level would be a good signal for a long position while a cross under the 50 level would be ideal for a short position.

Of course, we need to look for a confluence in trading (where more than one indicator/tool reveals the same trade signal). In this case, the tool I prefer is a trend line.

Before digging deeper into the core of this strategy, you should first switch the lower band value and upper band value to 0, instead of 30 and 70. After this adjustment, there is only one line (the mid-way line) in the RSI zone instead of two different lines as normal.

Now, let's discover how we can combine the RSI and the trend line to find a reliable trade signal on the chart.

This is the Cardano/Tether USD (ADA/USDT) 1-hour chart in July 2021. In this chart, the price was making a nice bearish move until a loss of momentum occurred at the end of the chart, with the price failing to form a lower low.

By drawing a trend line connecting the highs on the chart, we can easily identify a breakout. However, the breakout candlestick is not a momentum one. More importantly, the RSI reading has not surpassed the 50 level to the upside. In this case, we should observe the next candlestick(s) to have better confirmation of a trend reversal.

After two more candlesticks, the relevant RSI is now higher than 50. More ideally, the market forms a directional bullish candlestick which is longer than several previous ones. Entering a trade at the close of this candlestick would be a safer option.

As you can see in the picture below, the price went up nicely albeit having some consolidation periods along the way.

ADA/USDT
1-hour chart

Entry price

RSI above 50

At this point, some traders might raise concerns about the directional candlesticks and the RSI cross above the mid-way level. They may argue that a breakout coupled with an upward RSI higher than 30 is enough for a trade entry. Trading that way can bring about a better entry price and generate more profits.

While I agree with them to some extent, I must emphasize the unpredictability of financial trading. Unless you are a complete newbie, you may experience many negative feelings when the price goes against your expectations, although some signals say "yes" for a trade entry. I have seen many traders throw away a system that they used and were greatly proud of. The main reason for such a bad thing lies in the fact that they have not optimized their trade system enough. The strategy I introduce here is the one that I believe is safe and effective to generate long-term profits if applied appropriately.

In short, while I am not against a more aggressive method above, I want to emphasize you are taking on high risk when trading in the financial market. Whichever method you choose, you should and need to be comfortable using it.

Let's look at another example in an uptrend.

XRP/USDT
1-hour chart

RSI is above 50 line

This is the Ripple/Tether USD (XRP/USDT) 1-hour chart in September 2021. The market was in a nice uptrend at the beginning of the month, creating higher highs and higher lows without any signs of losing momentum. Yet, toward the end of the rally, it slightly broke the trend line drawn earlier. While a newbie may see it as an entry signal, there are some signs that say "no" to that.

First, the RSI is still above the mid-way line, and it is not steep enough to show the bears' strength in the market. Furthermore, the breakout candlestick is not a momentum one. These uncertainties make us watch the next price actions to better come up with a good decision. Here is what happened next:

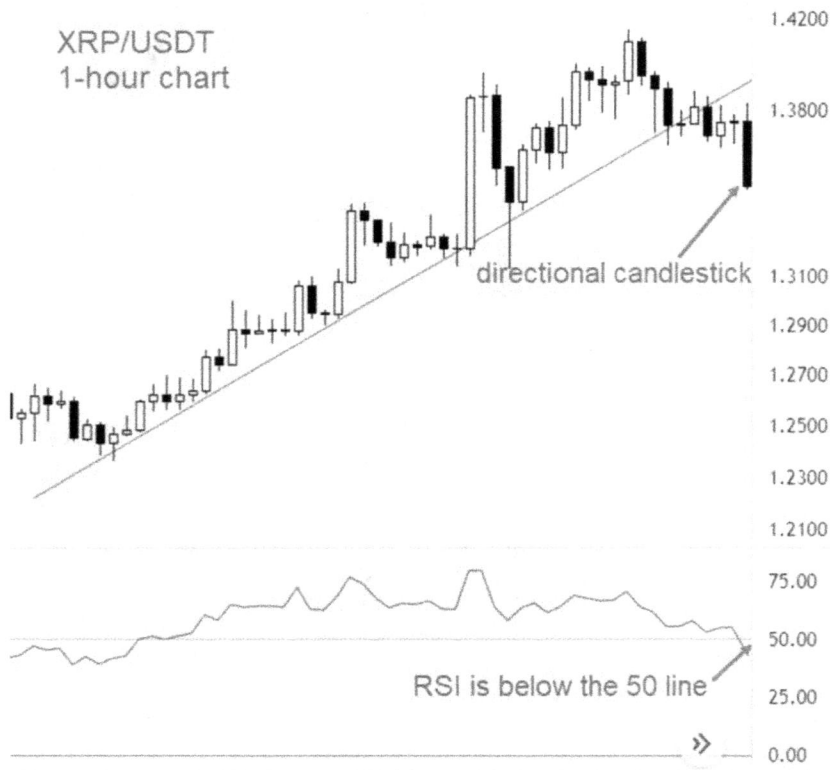

XRP/USDT
1-hour chart

directional candlestick

RSI is below the 50 line

After a few hours of waiting, we've now got what we need. A long bearish candlestick appeared on the chart, with its body nearly doubling the breakout candlestick. This is a much more reliable shift in momentum from upside to downside, indicating that the sellers were then ready to dominate the battle. Moreover, the RSI became steeper and crossed below the mid-way line to the downside, and we have one more confirmation signal to enter the trade at the close of the directional candlestick.

As you can see in the picture below, the price plummeted afterward.

XRP/USDT
1-hour chart

Entry price

1.4000
1.3500
1.3000
1.2500
1.2100
1.1700
1.1300
1.0837
1.0600
1.0300
1.0000
0.9720
75.00
50.00
25.00
0.00

12:00   6   12:00   7   12:00   8   12:00

Recommended time frame:

From 15-minute chart to daily chart (day traders and swing traders).

Key Takeaways:

- Always wait for a slight pullback to confirm an RSI divergence;

- Always treat RSI as a confirmation signal, and it must be combined with other tools;

- Use the 200 EMA to identify the prevailing trend correctly;

- A directional candlestick is highly recommended in finding a trade entry;

You can now understand the wide variety of benefits the RSI can bring about if applied correctly. The most important thing to note is that you should always treat RSI as a confirmation signal rather than the main trading tool. Seeking signals from other tools is highly recommended in financial trading. In the next chapter, you will discover the use of a fantastic tool which I have written a separate book about.

Chapter 9: Crypto Trading With Fibonacci Retracement

In trading, the concept "Fibonacci" refers to some tools that are used by nearly every trader in the financial market to determine the health of the trend as well as ideal entry and exit prices. As a trader, you may not need to master all Fibonacci tools to become profitable. In other words, some tools may be used more often than others by traders. In this chapter, I'll show you the tool that is probably used the most by Fibonacci traders in finding an entry: Fibonacci Retracement.

Introduction to the Fibonacci Retracement

Fibonacci Retracement is a tool for predicting the end of the price correction after a swing high or a swing low. Fibonacci retracement works via horizontal levels that indicate potential support and resistance. These levels are where there is a potential bounce back from the price.

Now you may wonder "Are there any indications that Fibonacci retracement levels can outperform normal support and resistance levels?" or "Why should we use the Fibonacci retracement levels instead of the normal support/resistance in some cases?"

I will answer these questions later in this chapter.

But first, let's have a brief overview of Fibonacci numbers and how they relate to the Fibonacci retracement levels used in financial trading.

The Fibonacci sequence is an interesting mathematical string first introduced by Leonardo Pisano Bogollo in the 13th century. The sequence starts with 0 and 1. From this, you just add the two previous numbers to get the next number, forming an infinite string like this:

0, 1, 1, 2, 3, 5, 8, 13, 21, 34, 55, 89, 144, 233, 377, 610, 987...

The interesting thing about this sequence occurs when you start to divide one number by its subsequent ones (excluding some first few numbers in the sequence). For example:

Dividing one number by its next number yields a ratio of roughly 0.618 (61.8 percent);

Dividing one number by the second number to the right yields a ratio of roughly 0.382 (38.2 percent);

Dividing one number by the third number to the right yields a ratio of roughly 0.236 (23.6 percent);

These results are used in defining some Fibonacci retracement levels that we'll discover more below: 61.8 percent level, 38.2 percent level, 23.6 percent level. Also, there are two more levels that are widely used to form standard 5-level Fibonacci retracements.

One is the 50% level. This level is not derived from the above sequence. However, it can play as a psychological barrier where buyers and sellers tend to react when the price approaches it.

Another level that is not derived from the above string is the 78.6 level. Adding such a level creates a sense of balance where there are two levels above the 50 percent line and two levels below the 50 percent line. Yet, its purpose is not restricted to creating a balance. As you progress on trading with Fibonacci, you will certainly notice price can sometimes touch this level and reverse.

Also, because Fibonacci levels are treated as support/resistance, we should treat them as zones instead of exact levels. The price may surpass the level or miss the level just a little bit, which is perfectly acceptable in trading.

Fibonacci is mostly used in anticipation of a continuation of the trend, and the Fibonacci retracement levels may signal the end of a pullback before the trend continues its previous direction.

Now, let's look at how Fibonacci levels look in a real chart:

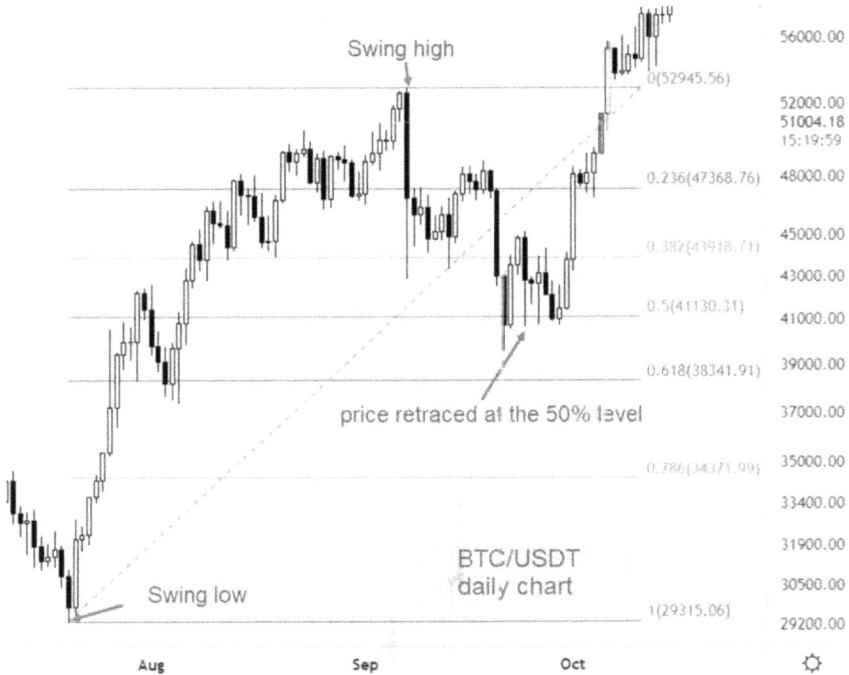

Swing high

0(52945.56)

0.236(47368.76)

0.382(43918.71)

0.5(41130.31)

0.618(38341.91)

price retraced at the 50% level

0.786(34371.99)

BTC/USDT
daily chart

Swing low

1(29315.06)

56000.00

52000.00
51004.18
15:19:59

48000.00

45000.00

43000.00

41000.00

39000.00

37000.00

35000.00

33400.00

31900.00

30500.00

29200.00

Aug   Sep   Oct

This is the Bitcoin/Tether USD (BTC/USDT) daily chart from July to October 2021. In this chart, the market was in an uptrend, hence Fibonacci is drawn from the swing low (the 100% percent level) to the swing high (the 0% level). After a rally, the price stabilized before resuming its original trend. A typical pullback ranges from the 23.6 percent level (the shallowest correction) to the 78.6 percent level (the deepest level). The market seldomly displays a 100% retracement level.

As you can see in the example above, the price made a correction to the 50 percent level before continuing its bullish momentum.

The most common levels to which the price may retrace are 38.2 percent, 50 percent, and 61.8 percent. These three levels together create the golden zone. Sometimes, the price may retrace to a shallower level at 23.6 percent or a deeper level at 78.6 percent. The 100 percent line is the maximum level that the counter move can still be considered a pullback.

If the price plummets and breaks below the 100 percent level (in a prevailing uptrend) or above the 100 percent level (in a prevailing downtrend), this tells us the counter move is not a pullback anymore. It signals that the reversal has officially initiated, and the market is ready to continue in the new trend.

Now you've had some rudimentary knowledge about how Fibonacci retracement works. Before showing you how to plot these retracement levels as well as how to utilize them to spot a reliable entry price, I would answer the question raised (by myself) at the beginning of the chapter: Why would Fibonacci outperform the normal support/resistance in some cases?

Let's look at the two examples below.

Example 1: Chainlink/Tether USD (Link/USDT) 1-hour chart

In this example, the market is in a strong downward trend, and we should look for a short entry. In this case, the best time for such entry should be at the end of a correction, as shown in the picture below:

Swing high

Short entry at the end of the pullback

Swing low

LINK/USDT
1-hour chart

As you may already know, a pullback may end at a key level. In this example, if we look further to the past, we will see that the end of the pullback aligns with a key level that rejects the price multiple times before. The picture below will clearly illustrate this.

Swing high

end of correction

Swing low

As we can see, the key level acts as support and resistance interchangeably during the period. In this example, the price "remembers" the key level and revisits it for a retest before the downtrend continues drastically.

As we all know, the cryptocurrency market is notorious for its wild movements during a short period. In these cases, finding a retest based on previous support/resistance would, on the whole, not be an easy task, especially for newborn cryptos in the market. Hence, using classic support/resistance would not be a good idea by traders in some cases.

Let's look at the picture below:

Example 2: VeChain/Tether USD (VET/USDT) 1-hour chart

On the left side of the chart, there are a lot of consecutive indecision candlesticks, and no key support/resistance is spotted. Toward the right of the chart, the price suddenly increased, forming a strong uptrend. We all know that the price may take a rest some time, but anticipating a support/resistance level based on a previous key level would be hard in this case.

On another angle, even though there is one previous support/resistance level on the chart, it may sometimes locate too deep, for example, around the 78.6 percent level. In a volatile market like crypto, the price may not retrace that deep, and looking for a correction to the prior key level could be hard from time to time.

This is where the Fibonacci retracements come into play. Let's see what happens when plotting Fibonacci lines on the chart.

The price reacts strongly at the 38.2 percent retracement level. Although having some difficulties, it made a successful advancement eventually.

VET/USDT
1-hour chart

0.15200
0.14800
0.14668
0.14400
0.14000
0.13700
0.13400
0.13100
0.12800
0.12600
0.12400

End of retracement

In short, Fibonacci retracements can help you to identify potential support/resistance in the absence of reference key levels in the past. More interestingly, what is needed in using the Fibonacci retracement tool is just a major swing high and a major swing low. That's why Fibonacci can outshine traditional support/resistance in some cases.

With that said, I won't say we should resort to Fibonacci retracements and forget about manually drawn support/resistance. If you are reading this section, you'll surely get my trading philosophy: Confluence in trading is super important. Hence, a combination of these two types of key levels is always recommended. Later in this chapter, we'll learn how to make the best use of this confluence.

Fibonacci Plotting

Now, let's discover how to draw Fibonacci retracements correctly on the chart.

Step 1: Choosing the Fib Retracement tool

If you are using tradingview.com, you can easily find the Fibonacci retracement tool on the left-hand side of the trading screen. Then, follow two simple clicks shown below:

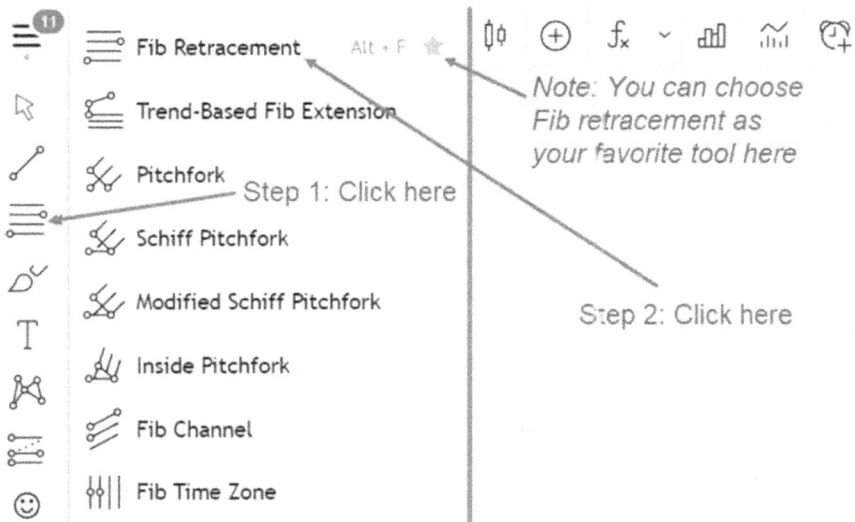

Fib Retracement   Alt + F ☆

Trend-Based Fib Extension

Pitchfork   Step 1: Click here

Schiff Pitchfork

Modified Schiff Pitchfork

Inside Pitchfork

Fib Channel

Fib Time Zone

Note: You can choose
Fib retracement as
your favorite tool here

Step 2: Click here

Tip: If you have chosen some tools as your favorite ones, you can have quick access to them by clicking on the star symbol at the bottom left of the screen as shown below.

Click here for a quick access to your favorite tool

17   Sep   15   Oct   15

1D 5D 1M 3M 6M YTD 1Y 5Y All

Stock Screener ∨   Text Notes   Pine Editor   Strategy Tester

Step 2: Identifying the swing high and swing low

The most important aspect in this step is identifying a major swing high and a major swing low. Let's discover how you can spot the swing high and swing low in two mini-steps below:

Identify a clear trend on the chart

To have a better picture of the prevailing trend, you can use the EMA 200 as shown in the previous chapter. In general, price movement below the 200 EMA could be considered a downtrend while price fluctuations above the 200 EMA would be the sign that an uptrend is prevailing. Yet, in many cases, identifying by the naked eye is enough. In the example below, it is clear that the market is in an uptrend.

Pick up the swing high and the swing low

In an uptrend like the example above, the swing low refers to the bottom point of the price swing while the swing high is the highest point before the retracement. Accordingly, the swing low could be identified easily, but a swing high can only be confirmed after a slight correction as shown in the picture above.

It's important that you choose the swing high and swing low uniformly, meaning that they can either be the extreme candlestick shadow points (lowest and highest shadow) or the extreme candlestick body points (lowest and highest closed price). On the other hand, using a shadow point for a swing low and the highest closed price for the swing high could lead to incorrect Fibonacci signals, especially in a highly volatile market.

Step 3: Plotting Fibonacci

After identifying the swing high and the swing low, all you need to do is place the cursor at the swing low and drag it to the swing high (in an uptrend), and vice versa (in a downtrend). The Fibonacci retracement levels will automatically appear on the chart as shown below.

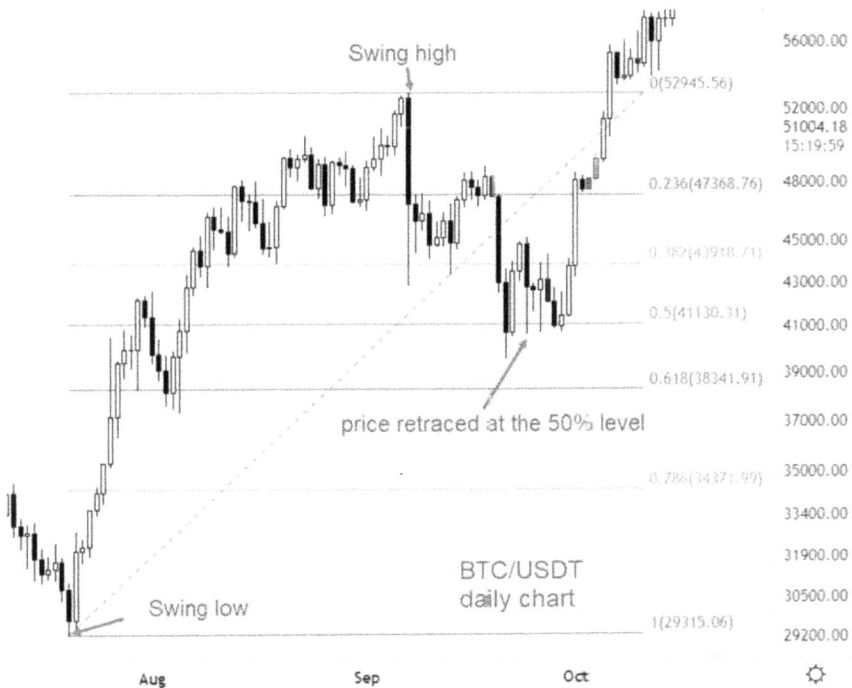

Trading with Fibonacci

Now that you have learned how to display Fibonacci levels on the chart, let's jump on the techniques for finding an entry, stop loss, and exit prices.

Principle:

Always look closely at how the price reacts at key Fibonacci retracement levels to better address which side is stronger in the market. A momentum candlestick is highly recommended, while a confluence would better stack the odds in your favor.

Until now, you may have mastered the mindset of avoiding any trade without a confirmation signal. In trading with Fibonacci retracement, what I pay attention to the most is how the price reacts at Fibonacci levels. Look at the Bitcoin/Tether USD (BTC/USDT) daily chart below:

This chart depicts the price action from July 2021 to September 2021. As we can see, after a nice rally to around $53,000, the price experienced a short consolidation period between the 23.6 percent level and the 38.2 percent level. Next, a strong bearish candlestick formed, poking below the 38.2 percent level. The price continued to approach the 50 percent level, and the 38.2 percent level was not respected anymore.

Now, all attention should be paid to how the price reacted at the 50 percent level.

The candlestick reactions say it all. As you can see, the price had a lot of difficulties breaking the 50 percent level to the downside. The sellers seemed to lose their energy, and this was when the bulls jumped in, pulling the price in the previous direction. This is clearly indicated by the big bullish candlestick that is longer than most of the previous candlesticks, breaking both the 38.2 percent level and the 23.6 percent level. This directional candlestick signals that the uptrend can resume afterward.

Let's sum up what we have on the chart until this time:

- Several strong price reactions at a key level (the 50 percent level);

- A strong directional candlestick pattern;

- Multiple retracement levels are broken;

Based on these price actions, there is a possibility that the price will continue in the overall direction following the directional candlestick. Now, we can be more confident to initiate a buy entry. As you can see in the picture below, the price went up nicely afterward:

BTC/USDT
Daily chart

Entry level

0(52930.72)

0.236(47343.25)

0.382(43886.59)

0.5(41092.86)

0.618(38299.12)

0.786(34321.60)

1(29255.00)

72000.00
66947.66
62000.00
56000.00
52000.00
50383.62
19:40:18
44000.00
41000.00
38000.00
35000.00
32500.00
30100.00
28100.00
26100.00

15   Aug   16   Sep   15   Oct   18   Nov

When trading Fibonacci retracements, it is much better to have a confluence in trading. In this chapter, let's explore the most common and powerful confluence I have been using for several years - the confluence between Fibonacci and support/resistance.

As we all know, the market often remembers the previous key levels and tends to respect such levels in many cases. In other words, it is when the price approaches the previous support/resistance levels that strong reactions may occur. Traders should watch these price reactions more closely because there is a probability of the price bouncing back from such key levels.

Below is an example of another uptrend concerning the Cardano/Tether USD (ADA/USDT) pair.

ADA/USDT
4-hour chart

In this chart, the price is making a nice upward movement before forming a slight pullback. Now, let's see how the price reacted at key levels when Fibonacci retracements are employed.

ADA/USDT
4-hour chart

After reaching the highest swing high, the price hovered around the 23.6 percent retracement level. As you can see from the picture, several indecision candlesticks appeared at this level, showing a balance between the bulls and the bears for that period. Toward the end of the chart, the market broke the 23.6 percent level to the downside, finding the 38.2 percent level. The price once again reacted drastically at this level but was unable to break the level.

Unlike the consolidation at the 23.6 percent level, the reactions at the 38.2 percent level ended with a big bullish candlestick. This candle is longer than most of the previous ones, breaking through the 23.6 percent level successfully. It suggests that the bulls were active again and had the power.

Interestingly, if we look back to the price actions in the past, the 38.2 percent retracement level aligns perfectly with a previous resistance level, which has now flipped into support. This officially forms a trading confluence, where at least two tools release the same signal on the chart. A confluence is expected to pave the way for a higher win-rate trade entry.

Now, let's sum up what signals we have at this point:

- The price reacted strongly at a key level (the 50 percent retracement level);

- The reaction appeared at a confluence level;

- The market forms a long bullish candlestick (a momentum/directional one) which broke the 23.6 percent level successfully;

This is an ideal opportunity to place a long position. Let's look at what happened next.

The price continued to skyrocket without any counterforce from the bears. You can see how powerful it is when a trade is backed up by a confluence.

Now, let's consider an example in a downtrend.

BNB/USDT
4-hour chart

Previous low

Latest low

In this example about Binance price, the latest swing is a downtrend. However, if you look at the left-hand side, the price was moving upward for a period before consolidating, and then a downtrend started. How do we know the downtrend, instead of an uptrend, is prevailing?

There are two reasons for that:

First, the latest swing low is lower than the previous major low in the uptrend, meaning that it cannot be a retracement of the uptrend (the maximum limit for a pullback is the 100 percent level).

Second, when employing the 200 EMA (the picture below), it is higher than the current price, indicating that the bears are dominating the market now. Hence, we should trade in the direction of the downtrend.

BNB/USDT
4-hour chart

200 EMA

Current price is
below the 200 EMA

Now that we have identified the prevailing trend in the market, let's plot Fibonacci levels and see how the price reacts when it approaches those levels.

This example shows you how the cryptocurrency market is notoriously volatile and unpredictable.

Starting from the swing low on the chart, the price corrected to the 50 percent Fibonacci retracement level. It was then constrained between the 23.6 percent and the 38.2 percent line before a long bearish candlestick appeared, breaking the 23.6 percent level to the downside.

While it might be the signal for a short entry, the price suddenly retested the 50 percent level once again. Those who placed a short position at the end of this bearish candlestick might end up in a loss. This depicts the unpredictability of the cryptocurrency market, where sometimes, you might suffer a loss although some market signals approve of a trade entry. No one can guarantee the success of any individual trade. Yet, you can minimize your loss in a losing trade by placing an appropriate stop-loss. We'll cover it in the next section.

Notice that when retesting, the price could not break the 50 percent level, indicating that it is a strong resistance level. Now, let's see what happened next on the chart.

BNB/USDT
4-hour chart

Another momentum candlestick

From the end of the retest level, the price fell quickly to the 23.6 percent line. At this level, the price reacted drastically, meaning the 23.6 percent level was a strong support level at that time. Luckily, toward the end of the chart, another long bearish candlestick formed, breaking the 23.6 percent level successfully.

Now, if you look at the two breakout candlesticks, you'll see one big difference concerning the way they break the support line. While the first one just slightly breaks the 23.6 percent level, the second one pokes through the level with 2/3 of its body below the line, meaning that the downward momentum in this candlestick is much stronger than the previous one.

To recap, the price showed several strong reactions at some key Fibonacci levels and a powerful candlestick broke below one strong key level. These are good and reliable signals to enter a short position.

As we can see in the picture below, the downtrend continued after the second momentum candlestick.

Stop loss and take profits

As can be seen in the last example, the crypto price is highly volatile. Even if you've collected a few reliable signals at the same time, chances are you may still encounter a loss. This is why stop-loss is a "must" on placing a trade entry. We will cover this aspect more in the last chapter of the book.

Setting a stop-loss:

• For more conservative traders:

A stop-loss can be put just below the end of the correction in an uptrend or above the end of the correction in a downtrend. Putting the stop-loss at this level may give the market enough room to breathe. A drawback of this method is you may not get an ideal risk/reward ratio sometimes.

● For risk-takers:

The stop-loss can be placed below the momentum candlestick in an uptrend or above that candlestick in a downtrend. In many examples in this book, you can see this type of stop-loss setting could safely hinder a loss. Yet, even if the stop-loss is hit, you've been successful in minimizing the loss incurred. One big advantage of this method is you can achieve a better risk/reward ratio compared to the previous method.

Setting a take-profit level:

Similar to the stop-loss level, where to set a profit-taking level depends on the tolerance degree in each trader.

● Day trading

If you are a day trader, you tend to prefer quicker profit-taking. Hence, an exit level at the 0 percent line can be placed.

With that said, being a day trader doesn't mean you should always close the trade within the day. If you believe in the strong momentum of the trend continuation, you may close your trade at a better price, ideally at next the support/resistance level, or when the market shows a loss of momentum.

● Swing trading or long-term trading

If you are a swing trader or a long-term trader, the 0 percent level may not seem attractive to you though it is considered a support/resistance level. In this case, you should look for a further support/resistance level or decide when the price shows certain tiredness in continuing the trend to identify the exit price. Being mainly a swing trader, I often opt for a risk/reward ratio of at least 1:3. More on that in the last chapter.

Key takeaways:

● Treat Fibonacci levels as areas, not exact price levels;

● Identify the long-term trend first before plotting Fibonacci levels (recommended: the 200 EMA);

● Choose swing high and swing low uniformly;

- Always watch the price reactions at Fib levels closely, and wait for at least one confirmation signal (ideally a directional/momentum candlestick breaking a key level) before initiating a trade;

- An area of confluence is recommended (but not a "must");

Recommended time frame:

Better used in 1-hour time frame and longer.

Fibonacci can be used in combination with a lot of other technical indicators, which further confirm your trade opportunities in the financial market.

In fact, Fibonacci has some other functions and I cannot cover all of them in this book. Yet, the Fibonacci retracement techniques I introduce in this book can be considered the most important tool among all in finding a good entry signal.

If you are interested in discovering more about Fibonacci techniques, my best-selling book "Secrets on Fibonacci Trading" can provide deeper understanding and techniques on the topic. In the next chapter, I will show you a very interesting trading lesson that can differentiate you from amateur traders out there in the cryptocurrency market.

Chapter 10: Dollar Cost Averaging (DCA) And The Art Of The Whales

What is Dollar Cost Averaging (DCA)

On the whole, the price of cryptocurrencies has been increasing for the past years. As a latecomer, one may find it hard to afford thousands of dollars for one crypto. At the time of this writing, one bitcoin is worth around $60,000 US dollars. Many people would wish they bought Bitcoin 10 years ago. Well, if we can roll back the time machine, then everyone else could all be millionaires now.

Yet, there is one way you can buy cryptocurrencies at a cheaper price: dollar cost averaging, or the DCA method. The logic here is simple: instead of investing all of your money in one cryptocurrency purchase, you buy a small amount at regular intervals. This technique often applies to large assets, which reduces the risk of the prices falling after the initial purchase. Generally, DCA may result in increased returns over time.

Another aspect is that DCA often works for long-term investments where the crypto tends to increase. Whereas, in the short-term, the price may often fluctuate, thus investors/traders may find it hard to determine which level is high and which level is low.

In short, DCA works the best with price fluctuating short-term and increasing long-term.

DCA helps investors make their trading decision less emotionally and more practically. Investors have the chance to buy more assets when the price gets lower. Moreover, they don't have to save enough money to be able to invest in a large cryptocurrency, such as Bitcoin or Ethereum. In a dynamic market like cryptocurrency where substantial ups and downs are common, waiting for a perfect time may earn you many good opportunities.

How does DCA work?

This technique includes two parts - the fixed investment and the regular interval to invest the same amount.

For instance: Let's say you intend to invest $100 to buy Bitcoin every month – the amount you can risk in the cryptocurrency market.

Accordingly, "$100" is the fixed investment, and "monthly" is the regular interval. As you keep investing $100 month by month, there may be some months you can buy at a better price due to market fluctuations. Doing this, if you have a four-year plan, you can consistently fund your investment and make purchases rather than identifying the exact time to buy a cryptocurrency.

Another important aspect lies in which cryptocurrency you choose to invest in, which requires deep analysis and commitment. DCA only works if you are loyal for one crypto asset for a long enough time. If you jump from one asset to another, the DCA method would not be effective in the long run.

In the next section, we will offer an example to show how DCA can be the difference between an amateur investor and a pro-investor.

Why Following Any Whale Could Be Super Risky

In today's social media boom, it is not difficult to see celebrities entering the crypto space. Elon Musk is one example who notoriously created chaos in the cryptocurrency market in 2021 via his tweets.

One concern is whether we should follow trade ideas offered by any authority or celebrity to maximize our profits and make a living with trading cryptocurrencies. Many of us may have a strong belief that authorities could not be wrong, and following them on buying and selling crypto could cut the corner and take us to financial success. Elon Musk did earn hundreds of millions of dollars in mid-2021 based on some opinions about Bitcoin. This can better solidify traders' beliefs in following some big players in the market.

Keep in mind that by mentioning Elon Musk here, I am not talking about himself alone. I am talking about any famous long-term investor or any well-known long-term trading firm you strongly believe in and pay great respect to in the trading industry. They are the ones who have had great success, the ones you believe cannot be wrong in their trading decisions.

But if you think you can blindly copy their trading decisions, you are in GREAT danger and are on the verge of blowing your account away.

Let's look at an example to better illustrate what I mean.

Let's say you know one trading guru called Elon Gates who has been trading for a long time. Elon is a well-known figure in the financial market and has gained great success during his trading career. He is exactly who you aim to be in your trading journey.

Now, Elon uses $60,000 (let's say 1% of his trading account) to buy 2 bitcoins at the price of $30,000. You have confirmed this and decide to follow his trading decision. However, you are so confident in this trade and decide to invest all of your money in the investment (all-in), hoping the price will double or triple soon.

However, things are not that promising. Strong fluctuations in the financial market cause the price to fall to the $20,000 mark, which temporarily blows 33.3% of your trading account away. You can't do anything but hope for the price to come back again.

Meanwhile, Elon continues to add to his position with 3 more bitcoins (with another $60,000). His account is still under control with a risk percentage of only 2%, not to mention that the second price is much better than the previous one.

After some time, the price continues to fall to a lower level at the $10,000 mark. This time, you are swearing about the market fluctuation (and swearing about Elon Gates himself) for sweeping 66.6% of your account away.

Guess what? Elon continues to buy 10 more bitcoins (this time with $120,000 of his asset).

At this point, the total amount of money Elon put in buying bitcoins is $240,000, and the number of bitcoins he owns is 15. On the contrary, you are losing 66% of your money due to the temporary downtrend of the market.

Now, let's say the market price increases by just $16,000 per bitcoin, Elon is break-even because most of his bitcoins were bought at a much lower price than your all-in price. On the other hand, even if the price increases to the $16,000 mark, you are still losing nearly half of your initial investment. This is not to mention that if you use leverage by just 1.5x, you would not have any chance of praying for the price to come back to the uptrend because you will have to either cut your losses early or see your account blown away.

For each price level above the $16,000 mark, Elon is making a profit while you still have to wait for the price to rise, rise more, and more. How long can you wait for the price to triple from $10,000 to $30,000, not to mention that if you can wait for such triple to occur, you would waste many more good opportunities during the same period?

By now, you may understand the reason you should not blindly follow anyone in financial trading in general and in crypto trading in particular. The difference I am talking about here is the "Financial Status". In the financial market, how you buy/sell is much more important than which price you buy/sell. To deliver a trading decision, each pro trader may have a detailed trading plan long before. Hence, without a specific idea of how you will execute in the market, you may put yourself in great danger.

In short, if you are not as rich as any Mr. Elon out there, you should forget about blindly following his trading decisions at all costs.

Note: This is a hypothetical example to show you the importance of trade management. In reality, the market may not make such a deep fall, and you might not be patient enough to wait for the price to come back from the $10,000 bottom. Real trading is more complex with lots of news and rumors every day, which may further affect your trading decisions. Yet, in all circumstances, equipping yourself with adequate skills and techniques is of prime importance in being successful in the financial market.

Chapter 11: Stop-Loss Optimization

Until now, we have mentioned the concept of stop-loss many times concerning each strategy we apply. Simply put, stop-loss is used to limit the potential loss of a trade by automatically liquidating the assets once the price hits a specific target. A disciplined and well-organized trader would always use stop-loss in each of his trades.

Stop-loss is considered insurance in trading, preventing your loss from becoming bigger. We all take losses in financial trading, period. Yet, how you manage loss defines how successful you will be in trading. A consistently profitable trader would not let losses run beyond control.

Setting a good stop-loss requires careful analysis of market behaviors, otherwise, a loss may become bigger than it should be. In this chapter, we will talk more about different methods of stop-loss setting that can be useful in both keeping your trades under control and letting your profits run.

Setting stop-loss with Average True Range (ATR)

What Is The Average True Range?

The Average True Range (ATR) is a technical indicator that measures the volatility of the market over a certain period. It's displayed as a line that indicates the magnitude of price movement depending on the time frame used. Take a look at the example below:

The ATR indicator's upward or downward direction will depend on how the price moves. For example, if the price moves get larger, the indicator will show an upward direction and vice versa. Yet, ATR is not designed to predict the direction of the price on the chart. There is no ATR to tell you whether the trend may continue or reverse soon, rather its function lies mainly on identifying the volatility caused by gaps and the movement range of the candlesticks.

In a trading chart, the ATR value is located at the bottom left of the trading screen. When you move the cursor along the ATR line, the ATR value will automatically change because the calculation range for determining the value has been changed.

There are two components in calculating the ATR value. The first one is the timeframe. For example, on the five-minute chart, a new ATR reading is calculated every five minutes. On a 4-hour chart, ATR is calculated on a 4-hour basis.

The second component is the period used in measuring the volatility of the market. The default period setting is 14. However, you can get more signals by reducing the number of periods, and vice versa. Normally, I won't change the default setting value.

This indicator is used in day trading more often, helping day traders confirm when they might want to initiate a trade, or where they might opt for a stop-loss order. In this section, we will focus on the role of ATR in setting a stop-loss.

Using ATR in setting a stop-loss

To use the ATR, you need to first set up the indicator on your platform. Similar to some indicators introduced before, we follow three simple steps in displaying the ATR value on the chart.

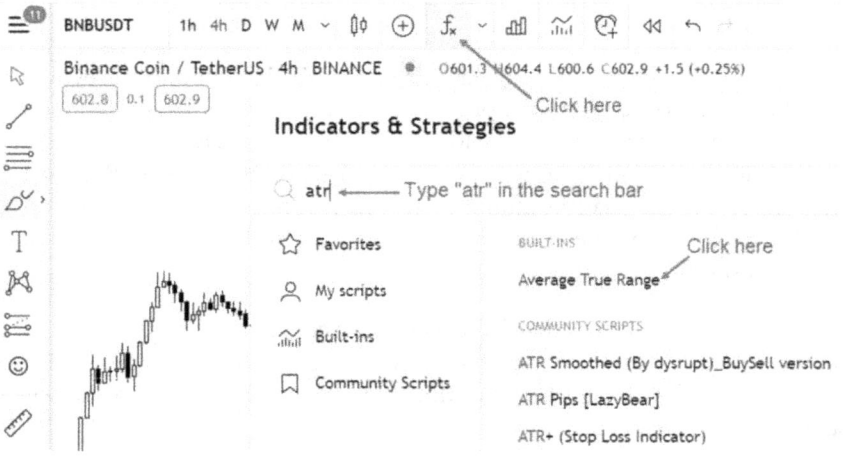

BNBUSDT 1h 4h D W M ˅

Binance Coin / TetherUS 4h · BINANCE ● O601.3 H604.4 L600.6 C602.9 +1.5 (+0.25%)

602.8 0.1 602.9

Click here

Indicators & Strategies

atr ←——— Type "atr" in the search bar

☆ Favorites

BUILT-INS   Click here

My scripts

Average True Range

Built-ins

COMMUNITY SCRIPTS

Community Scripts

ATR Smoothed (By dysrupt)_BuySell version

ATR Pips [LazyBear]

ATR+ (Stop Loss Indicator)

Now, let's discover how to use the ATR in setting a stop-loss in your trading.

First, let's come to an example that may be familiar to many traders. In the example below, let's say you are about to take a long position and choose a tight stop-loss as shown below.

BNB/USDT
4-hour chart

Entry price

Stop-loss

Unfortunately, the price starts to make a lower retest, hitting your stop-loss, and from that, it resumes its upside momentum dramatically as shown in the picture below.

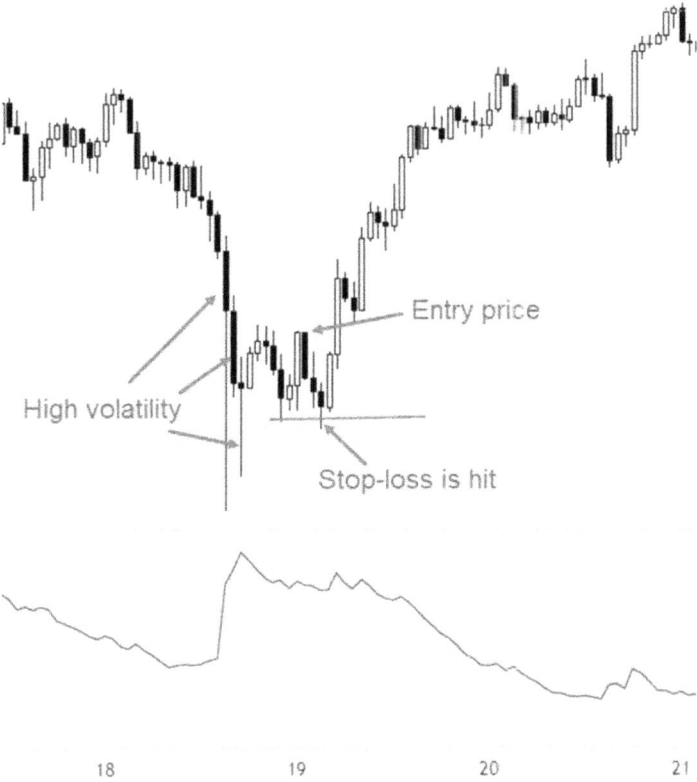

We all know that stop-loss hitting is unavoidable, and there is no magic to help us avoid this. However, there is a technique that can give us a better view of the market fluctuation. From that, you may have more information to choose the final price for the stop-loss order.

Still in the example above, by looking at some previous candlesticks before the momentum one, we can see strong fluctuations in the market price. They are illustrated by very long candlestick shadows, signaling a heated battle between the bulls and the bears toward the end of the downtrend. A sensible trader should take notice of this, and putting a wider stop-loss could be a good idea.

Now, let's see what the ATR value tells us in this case.

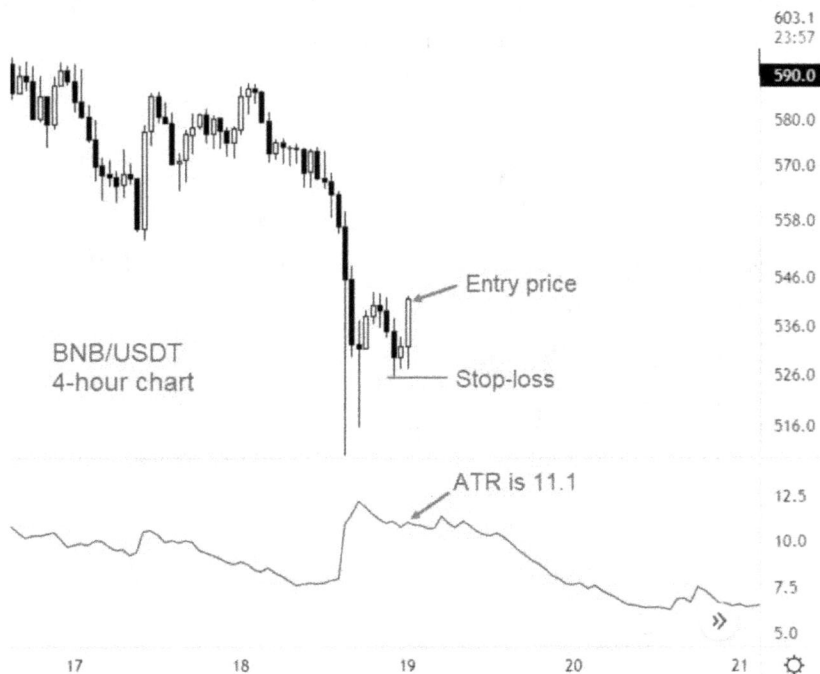

BNB/USDT
4-hour chart

Entry price
Stop-loss
ATR is 11.1

Note that the corresponding ATR to the momentum candlestick is 11.1, meaning that the average price movement range within the last 14 periods is $11.1. Yet, we don't use the exact price magnitude for setting a stop-loss. Notice that the market has witnessed wild fluctuations recently, hence, a stop-loss of two times the ATR value (around 22) is more suitable. By widening the stop-loss in a more volatile market, we can avoid some unexpected losses while letting profits run in many cases.

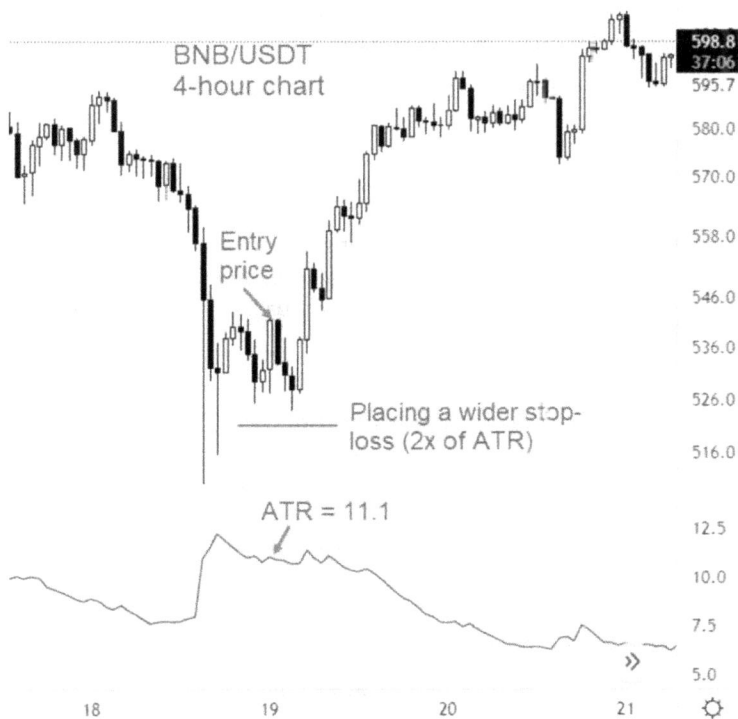

BNB/USDT
4-hour chart

Entry
price

Placing a wider stop-
loss (2x of ATR)

ATR = 11.1

Using the ATR in identifying your stop-loss can be a good idea because it measures the volatility of the market. Each market has its respective degree of price fluctuation. If the market is volatile and you choose a tight stop-loss, it is likely to be hit. In contrast, if the market has less volatility and you choose a tight stop-loss, it would be more reasonable.

Moreover, within the same market, the volatility degree might be different over time. In the example above, the market has been experiencing a volatile period, hence, using the exact ATR value might not be a safe option. By placing a stop-loss at a level twice the ATR value below the entry price, we allow the price more room to breathe before continuing in the prevailing direction.

Here comes the suggestion in choosing a stop-loss based on the ATR value:

A stop-loss can be placed at twice the ATR value under or below the entry price (depending on whether you are in a long or a short position);

Note: This is my suggestion in trading in the cryptocurrency market. There is no right or wrong answer in choosing a stop-loss for a trade. If you don't advocate this, adjust it and see how your method works over time.

Remember the art of entering a trade based on the close of the directional/momentum candlestick? Doing this reduces the possibility of the price coming back and sweeping the stop-loss. By combining this with the ATR value, we are enhancing the security of our trade execution even more.

Let's move to another example of using the ATR.

BTC/USDT
1-hour chart

Entry price

Stop-loss twice
the ATR value

ATR value is 695

In this example, to the left of the chart, there are consecutive bearish candlesticks, indicating the strength of the bears. However, as the price approaches the $30,000 level – a powerful support level – the bulls jumped in and pushed the price higher. Yet, traders should be conservative considering the strong downward momentum before. This is the reason why we should not place a trade until the third consecutive bullish candlestick in this case.

Notice the corresponding ATR value of 695 in this case. As we can see, putting a stop-loss at twice the ATR value below the entry level can give the market just enough room to breathe before the subsequent rally.

Keep in mind that to better secure your trading account, instead of retaining your initial stop-loss level, you can consider moving your stop-loss if the price moves favorably with your analysis. In other words, you would continue to raise the stop-loss until it is hit by a pullback. This requires closely monitoring the trading chart to keep up with each market fluctuation.

For example, you take a long position at $1,000 and the ATR is 10. You are a conservative trader and choose a stop-loss of 20 (two times the ATR). The price increases to $1,050 and the ATR remains the same, hence you can move your stop-loss to $1,030. Now you have at least $30 of profit because you would either move your stop-loss above (if the price keeps rising) or remain the same level until the stop-loss is triggered.

Trailing your stop-loss with ATR-based indicator

Another way to use the ATR as a trailing stop-loss while requiring less time spent on the screen is by using the Chandelier Stop. This indicator is based on the ATR value. The main objective of using the Chandelier Stop is to signal a potential trend reversal after a dominant trend.

During a low volatility market, many traders tend to set a tighter stop-loss, helping them to get the most of the trend movement before a reversal. Whereas, during higher volatility, traders may opt for a wider stop-loss to avoid being hit by the market fluctuations.

Due to the close relationship between the volatility and the stop-loss placement, Chandelier Stop can be used to protect traders from an abrupt reversal in trading.

Setup: It is completely similar to the other technical indicators, just type "Chandelier Stop" in the search bar, and done.

The principle in using the Chandelier Stop is simple: when the price hits the line, you close the trade. This could be the start of a trend reversal.

Let's look at the example below.

In this example, the market is in a strong downtrend, with consecutive lower highs and lower lows. At the end of the swing, the price hit the Chandelier Stop, signaling a reversal of the trend. An exit at the intersection between the Chandelier Stop and the price could be a suitable decision.

Note: There is no guarantee that a reversal will happen when the above hit appears, and such a hit should be treated as a reference signal only. In some cases, the price continues going with the prevailing trend.

Trailing your stop-loss with the 200 Moving Average

What is a Moving Average (MA)

In the financial market, a moving average (MA) is an indicator that is often used in technical analysis. The main objective of an MA is to smooth out the market price by constantly updating the average price over a certain period. Via the calculation of the averaged price, short-term fluctuations of the market price in any time frame are considerably reduced.

Technically speaking, the MA is calculated to identify the trend direction or support and/or resistance levels. It is a lagging indicator, meaning it is determined based on past prices.

In the previous chapters, we learned about the EMA 200, which is also a type of moving average. Besides the use as a long-term trend determination signal, the moving average can be treated as running support/resistance, giving traders an option in managing their trades.

The MAs are calculated based on a certain number of periods. The greater the period is, the less sensitive the indicator is. Understandably, the 200 MA will be lagger than the 50 MA because it contains more price data than the 50 MA. These two moving averages are considered the most widely used by investors and traders in trading many types of assets, including cryptocurrency trading.

In this section, we will focus on the 50 MA and the 200 MA and use them as the basis for trailing stop-loss effectively. While predicting the future price moves is next to impossible, using these two moving average lines may greatly help you with protecting your profits and letting them run.

First, let's look at how these two moving averages can play as great support and resistance level:

As you can see, as long as the price remains above the 50 MA and the 200 MA, the uptrend remains strong. An uptrend is represented by a clear upward movement of the Moving Average (MA).

Principle: In an uptrend, you set the stop-loss just below the 50 MA or the 200 MA and raise it based on price movements.

If you want to follow the price more closely and set a tighter stop-loss, then the 50 MA could be a good option. On the other hand, if you want to monitor the price on a bigger movement range, consider using a looser one like the 200 MA.

Whenever you want to secure your unrealized profits from highly volatile price actions, just move the stop-loss below the latest moving average on the chart.

There are also times where you may want to divide your positions into short-term and long-term ones. In this case, you'll need to plot both the 50 MA and the 200 MA on the chart. The 50 MA will be used to trail short-term stops while the 200 MA is for long-term stops trailing.

Take a look at the chart below for a better illustration:

160.00
130.00
100.00
89.92
13:59:5
Tight trailing stop   64.00
52.00
42.00
Loose trailing stop   34.00
26.00
200 MA
21.00
17.00
50 MA
AVAX/USDT   13.50
Daily chart
10.50

Aug   Sep   Oct   Nov   Dec

Chapter 12: Exiting The Trade: Be Flexible

From Chapter 6 to Chapter 9, we have learned a few ways of identifying the exit price for a trade. In this chapter, we will discuss another aspect of closing a trade: how we can exit a trade to optimize profits amid market volatility.

Each trader may have his/her own exit plan. Yet, one exit plan may be suitable for one trader, but not for others. This is the reason why choosing different trading plans in different market conditions is important to the profitability of the trade. Put differently, we should be flexible in exiting trades.

This chapter will present four different exit options for you to choose from. At the end of the chapter, you can understand what to do and what not to do in terms of profit-taking in the financial market.

Also, note that there are no "right" or "wrong" answers in choosing an exit strategy that suits you. In other words, each strategy has its pros and cons, and it is your responsibility to determine which one suits you best in each circumstance. Choosing an appropriate exit strategy depends on many factors, and before applying the techniques I'll share below, you should understand these three things:

You need to know your goals: Is it to make only 10% repeated multiple times? Or is it doubling or tripling your holding? Or is it long-term holding?

It takes time to make the best use of one strategy. Hence, do not rush and hope for a quick return. You should be patient and practice continuously until you find the one(s) that work best for you in each circumstance.

It's all about probability: Sometimes, your strategies work well, but sometimes they don't. Just accept this, and remember: Trading is about how much you make when you're right and how much you lose when you're wrong.

Now, let's move to four different methods of exiting a trade:

Strategy 1: Exit by return

The first strategy is exiting by return. Let's say you take a long position in Ripple (XRP) when it is at one dollar. Based on some techniques, you identify that the two-dollar mark will be a possible step and brings you decent money (100 percent in profit). In this case, you must stick with the price target you have set, ideally by writing them down as a way of reminding you each time you look at the chart.

The reason for that is you can easily be affected by price movement, external news about the potential of the coin going to the moon, etc. When the price nearly reaches the two-dollar benchmark, you may become euphoric and forget about the initial exit price that you aim at. Instead of taking profit at the $2 level, you hope for the price to reach $3, $4, $5. Even when there is a strong bounce back in the market, you still hope for it to resume as soon as possible (because it **used to be** very bullish). Your emotions and greed have now taken over, driving your thoughts and actions in a very different way to what you planned before.

This is a common story to most newbies, I'm sure of that.

The lesson here is if you have set a price target for your trade, follow it at all costs. You should be calm and relaxed if XRP goes higher than $2. There is no need for any regret. Instead, you should be happy because your target is achieved and you made a profit.

Strategy 2: Exit at different price targets

This technique provides more flexibility in exiting trades. For example, you buy Ethereum (ETH) at the price of $4,000 and your price target is $10,000. However, instead of selling all of your ETH at $10,000, you divide your exit volume into five different sections. For example, you will sell 0.2 ETH in your investment portfolio when the price reaches each of these price levels: $8,000, $9,000, $10,000, $11,000, $12,000. When you complete all the sell orders, you will be sitting on $10,000 in cash.

Now, you might be asking why we don't sell the whole ETH at the price of $12,000. Simply put, there is no guarantee that the price will reach the $12,000 mark. Also, do you remember what we learned in the previous technique? You should pay respect to the price target you set before. If your target is $10,000, stick to it. Do not move it to $12,000 or more because you are getting distracted from your target.

The idea of using multiple profit-taking levels is you can lock in and secure your profits along the way. Doing this, when the market unexpectedly makes a dip, at least you have taken some profits. In case the market dips lower, you can purchase more Ethereum with the profits you have accumulated. On the whole, it is a win-win situation, because it's very hard to time the market fluctuation and try to catch tops and bottoms. It is much more advisable to make profits from some large moves within the whole trend, and it's more than enough.

Again, before applying this strategy, you should be able to identify your target price based on some independent tools such as support/resistance levels, or trend lines. Determining a random price target may not be a good idea to combine with this strategy.

Strategy 3: Dollar Cost Average Out

In the previous chapter, we learned about using Dollar Cost Average to find some buy positions. But it can also be a good way of exiting a trade as well. The principle is simple: Instead of selling your entire position at one time, you divide your exit phases on a regular basis.

There are two components within this strategy: the timeline and the fixed exit percentage.

For example, say you believe in the four-year cycle of Bitcoin and assume the peak of the market could be around December. This means that you should be prepared to exit the trade toward the end of the year. Let's assume the time you start to exit out of your trading portfolio is September. That is, starting in September, you close your trade every week on its way to the anticipated top in December. Because there are around 17 weeks from September to December, you may choose to close around 5% each time.

If you think September is too early, you can start in October. Let's say you want to exit every two weeks, which turns out to be 6 exits in total. This time, you can choose to close around 15-20 percent of your entire portfolio each time until your crypto is 100 percent sold out.

In short, you would decide the timeline for your strategy, both in terms of exit duration period and the frequency of your selling orders. There is no "right" or "wrong" in choosing a timeline. From that, you will decide a fixed percentage for each round of selling.

Strategy 4: Exiting by portfolio

Exiting by portfolio depends on your financial goals. In other words, it's well connected with your initial objective in joining the crypto market.

- Is it to make some money to buy a new car?

- Is it to pay off some debt?

- Is it to buy some equipment for your business?

The reason you enter the market is important. It should not be covering your regular expenses (i.e arising on a weekly or monthly basis). The reason should be a financial goal that allows a certain lagging time for you and no specific deadline is attached.

The cryptocurrency market is known as a very volatile market with substantial ups and downs. One advantage of this is that you can reap huge profits without using leverage (leverage is always notorious for its danger to a newbie's trading account). However, if you rush into making more and more money in the shortest time possible, chances are you would lose all of your initial investment.

After finding the reason as well as the target profit, you must stick to it. For example, you invest $20,000 buying Ethereum with a target profit of $10,000. If the market goes favorably and such target is achieved, then you should lock in such profits and be happy to serve your purposes. Like I mentioned in previous chapters, the market operates 24/7, and the price can go higher, even 2x or 3x. Just accept it because your financial goal is all you think of before you purchased crypto.

Now that you have grasped the four methods of exiting the trades, here are some tips you can apply to gain the best efficiency in your trading:

- Persevere and be flexible

The financial market is not about black and white answers. None of the strategies above is superior to the others. You should try to find yourself the most suitable strategy each time you make an investment.

One mistake that beginners often make is to rely on other (experienced) traders on when to enter and exit. It is understandable at the beginning of their trading career because they should learn how to invest or trade from experienced ones. The more they learn, the better.

However, problems may arise when many of them still rely on others to execute their trades after years. They could not navigate the market and establish any trading system, including exit techniques. We call this situation "the lack of control in trading". You must persevere in this journey.

Another aspect is that you should be flexible in applying exit techniques. There is no fixed way of opening and closing trades. Market conditions are different over time, and your investment goals could also be different each time. Hence, the way you apply each method can be different in each circumstance. In short, flexibility is key.

- Choose to hold

Sometimes, you may find it better to hold instead of getting out of your position. In the financial market, each person has their financial status and goals.

Some investors enter the market to make profits regularly. They use leverage in their trading, and to them, just a small price movement could be enough to bring about a decent profit. They are the ones who don't choose to hold their cryptocurrency long-term.

On the other hand, some investors participate in the financial market in general and in the cryptocurrency market in particular without any urgency of making profits. They might have an abundance of money and find some ways of putting their capital in for long-term profits. These investors may hold their crypto longer than crypto traders, i.e., 5 years, 10 years, or even more.

If you belong to this group, congratulations because chances are you are generating a decent flow of income outside the crypto space. In this case, there is no urgent need for you to liquidate your investment any time soon. On the other hand, if you believe taking risks would interest you more, consider using leverage with a part of your trading portfolio, and leave the remaining safe and sound for a long-term perspective.

In short, throughout this chapter, we learned about different techniques in how you exit your trade/ investment. While finding the exit price requires more technical analysis, the art of exiting entails a deep understanding of personal goals as well as flexibility in coping with the market.

PART THREE

RISK MANAGEMENT BLUEPRINTS, AND MORE

IN THIS PART

Discover the five elements in risk management that are even more important than the trading techniques;

Chapter 13: Risk Management Methods

Crypto investing, like any other form of investment, requires risk management strategies for both long-term and short-term investments. Most advisers will tell you that given crypto's famous volatility, taking measures against risk is a must. Although this is true, it is also not exclusive to Bitcoin or crypto in general. All asset classes under the sun are volatile, risky, and unpredictable. Moreover, they are subject to untrained usage, speculation, and error. For these reasons, I believe you should treat risk in crypto the same way you would with any other form of investment asset: with a lot of respect, but without exaggerating either.

To properly understand how to be cautious when trading cryptocurrencies, it is essential to grasp a key idea that goes beyond the mere volatility debate. Yes, crypto is volatile, but why is that? It's all about the mechanics of volatility itself because volatility is one of the most salient characteristics of cryptocurrency markets. Although it is probably the reason why it's so famous and why traders use crypto to generate profits, the instability or crypto prices can also play against traders' expectations. Volatility has truly made and unmade fortunes overnight.

The mechanics are as follows: Everyday fiat currencies have an endless supply—not because they're abundant or scarce, but because they are artificial assets and central banks can issue them at will. Real-life assets, by contrast, have a limited supply because there can only ever be so much of them. In this realm, you have, for example, gold or any other precious metal, along with many other assets like lumber or wheat. These assets all have a limited supply because they are tangible, and up until a decade ago, only tangible assets were capable of having that property.

But then along came crypto and changed everything. Just like fiat currencies, crypto is an artificial, intangible asset, yet at the same time, it does have a limited supply. No one has the authority to say how much of it there will be, and its supply limit is hardcoded into the design itself. Of course, some altcoins have tweaked this somewhat, but in general, they tend to have supply capped at some point.

This is the reason some have come to consider Bitcoin a form of digital gold. Because it is so scarce and has no regulating body at its core, Bitcoin is especially sensitive to changes in supply and demand as well as speculation. It's the same as a cup of coffee: It is so small that the slightest hint at excess sugar could ruin it all. You have no room for error. When it comes to currencies, you generally want a much larger amount that gives you a chance to add more of it and not suffer such drastic changes. This is the case, for instance, with fiat currencies. There is inflation, but nothing as volatile as crypto's volatility. That's the sweet spot crypto has yet to reach to become proper money.

Besides hacking attacks, which you can only take partial measures against, risk management is all about addressing crypto's volatility. In other words, it's about reading supply and demand dynamics in a small cup of coffee. There are specific blueprints for you to adopt against risk in crypto investing.

Stop-loss

As I mentioned, whichever strategy you apply in trading, there's always a possibility of a loss in each trade, not to mention cryptocurrency trading is an extremely volatile market. All you can hope to achieve with your trading strategies is to maximize gains and minimize losses. When it comes to an instrument that can limit your losses to a minimum level, it's all about a stop-loss order.

A stop-loss, commonly abbreviated as S/L, is an order you can place to close a trade if it reaches a certain undesired price point. It's a contingency to bail before the ship sinks completely. The main purpose of this order is to limit losses during an unsuccessful trade, which comes in handy when a prediction of yours is wrong. The outcome still has an impact, but you only risk a small capital percentage as opposed to risking it all.

When the level of your stop-loss order is reached, your contract is immediately and automatically terminated. This closes the possibility of giving any second chances to an asset, thereby protecting your investment capital and putting an objective tone to your most deeply ingrained investment practices.

For instance, let's say you were to place a stop-loss order at a price level that is 2% lower than the price a cryptocurrency had when you first bought it. What would follow is you'd be limiting your losses up to just a 2% price difference between the entry and the stop-loss levels. It sounds pretty cool, right? And to top it off, it's worth pointing out that stop-loss orders are famous for not having any additional fees. In a way, we could say they work as a form of feeless insurance.

The primary effect this instrument could have in your own investing is it will relieve you of emotional weaknesses. An emotion-free temper is an important asset to have because markets are driven by forecasts and expectations, so avoiding at least some of that is rare. Imagine, for example, that your emotions were telling you to keep believing in a position you opened, and that is unquestionably going down. If you follow these emotions, you will end up losing money. In other words, a stop-loss frees you from unrealistic expectations that will eventually blow up your trading account.

Moreover, a stop-loss order will do as it was told previously, no matter what your emotions are at the moment. It allows you to implement the "set it and forget it" scheme, where you are given the freedom to walk away from your trading screens to work on another business, enjoy some hobbies, or get some exercise, etc. You won't have to sit glued to the trading chart all day only to suffer from negative trading emotions constantly.

There are multiple stop-loss strategies, and choosing which one depends on a number of factors, from which time frame you trade, which types of trader you are, and which market signals you are opting for. While you should be flexible in testing them and measuring their effectiveness over time, remember not to make things too complicated in each trade you take.

Risk vs. profit ratio

This risk/reward ratio is used to visualize the correlation between a potential loss and target profit. The risk is identified by the distance between the open price and the stop-loss order. Meanwhile, the profit target indicates a price level where a trader can get out of a trade with a nice profit. Simply put, the risk/reward ratio is achieved by dividing potential loss by potential profit.

In any case, our objective is to keep the potential loss smaller than the profit so that each time the price hits the stop-loss, your loss is minimized. A higher risk/reward ratio means for every loss that may occur, you can have a chance of achieving a much larger profit.

Suppose, for example, that you bought crypto for $4,000, which is more or less the current market price of Ethereum. As you know about the general volatility of crypto, you expect to resell this cryptocurrency after its price has risen at least a thousand more. At the same time, suppose you're open to a loss of up to $250 in case things go wrong. So, the way to calculate this ratio is by dividing your expected profit and your margin of loss. In this hypothetical case, we'd have a risk/profit ratio of 1:4.

As I mentioned throughout the book, even if we've applied the most effective systems in trading, there is always the possibility of losses due to market volatility and unpredictability. The magic good risk/reward ratio may not be felt short-term, but its effects, in the long run, are unquestionably huge. A ratio of 1:3, for example, means that for every winning trade you have, you can suffer up to three similar losing ones without negatively affecting your balance account.

Concerning the ideal risk/reward, I always emphasize a rate of at least 1:2, though a minimum ratio of 1:3 would mostly be applied in my trades. Yet, there is no fixed rule because choosing a risk/reward ratio also depends on the trading style and the strategy we use.

Understanding the roles of a good risk/reward ratio not only saves you from constant risks in the market but also determines whether you are going to be a successful trader in the long term.

Position Sizing

One of the most frequently asked questions among people interested in crypto investing is: "if this is my first time, how much should I invest?"

The question addresses an important aspect in trading any assets: position sizing.

Position sizing refers to the size of the position within a particular portfolio or the amount of money that the investor/trader is going to put into the trade. It determines how many cryptos you would purchase; from that, you can better control the risks and maximize returns. Good position sizing depends on a number of factors, including account size and account risk.

Account size: While this may seem a redundant step, it truly matters. If you are a beginner, it can help you allocate your capital to different strategies and even different cryptos, all based on your analysis (more on that in the next section). By doing this with each strategy you apply, you can better track your progress while reducing the risk of trading/investing too much. In this way, successfully determining your account size entails monitoring your account balance closely for allocation purposes.

Account risk: The second element in position sizing is determining your level of risk for each trade you take. Simply put, it is the percentage of your available capital you are willing to risk on each trade.

In the traditional financial trading world, there is a golden percentage each trader should grasp: 2%. It says traders should not risk more than 2% of their trading account in a single trade. Remember that this figure is applied for traditional markets and tailored to less volatile assets than the cryptos. Hence, a little twist may be needed to cope with this characteristic of the market.

So, if you just started in crypto trading, it's better to adopt a more conservative approach than the above option. Hence, a risk percentage of 1% should be considered, meaning that you should not risk more than 1% of your trading capital in any single trade. By doing this, when the trade goes poorly, and your stop-loss is hit, you only lose 1% of your trading account. For example, if you have a $20,000 trading account, and the 1% rule is applied, you won't risk more than $200 per trade ($20,000 x 1%). Doing this, even if you've made ten consecutive wrong trading decisions, you only lose $2,000, which is 10% of your account.

Again, it's not about right or wrong in choosing 1% or 2%. As a crypto beginner, you should start with a safer option and then consider increasing the risk level once you've got the hang of the crypto market. Conversely, the all-in style (where you put all your money into one or very few trades) is the quickest way to ruin your trading account.

In short, while market analysis could be seen as the core aspect in trading any type of assets, position sizing is a supplemented aspect, but compulsory insurance in any trade you take. Along with stop-loss, it prevents your trades from getting worse and protects your account for long-term profitability. Start wrapping your trades with these barriers of insurance, ideally with cryptos you feel the most comfortable trading based on your careful analysis, and see what happens over time.

Portfolio diversification

Every investment course will give you their version of this. You will often hear the expression: Don't put all your eggs in one basket. If and when you identify great individual investments, you should allocate resources to take full advantage of them. However, conducting a full portfolio restructuring on account of such opportunities is an exaggeration. No single opportunity can ever be good enough to give up an entire portfolio.

This brings us into a sensitive section of risk management, which is that the best protection against risk isn't insurance but simply a well-rounded portfolio distribution. Same as you'd find in regular finance, a crypto portfolio must have a bunch of sacred cows, as it were, and then a smaller collection of riskier ventures. For instance, the sacred cows could be a number of cryptocurrencies that have been consistently on the rise and whose market caps look robust. On the other hand, riskier investments could be relatively reliable Initial Coin Offerings (ICOs) or less well-known cryptocurrencies. The integrity of your portfolio isn't in any one of these investments, but rather on the whole of them working as a team.

An important lesson can be drawn from this. In crypto, there is no such thing as one single golden asset class that will fit all your needs. As an investor, you shouldn't think of yourself as a hunter in search of the right prey but rather as a cattle rancher who always overviews several projects at once.

When an investor diversifies into different projects, every individual investment has a reasonable chance of having either good or bad outcomes. However, the entire group is less prone to failure because it's highly unlikely for all investments to yield a bad outcome simultaneously. Some will be profitable, and some won't, but the portfolio as a whole will always stay afloat. Better still, if you pick every crypto investment carefully, the chances for failure will reduce even more.

For example, the crypto-verse offers a handful of big, well-established cryptocurrencies. These probably are why you heard of crypto in the first place, but they're also somewhat settled by now. As a new investor, your priority should be picking new promising altcoins with a chance for growth and putting a stake in several of these to increase your chances for profit. At the same time, you should worry about stability, so it'd be wise to have some of the major cryptocurrencies as your sacred cows and resort to stablecoins to preserve value.

Patience

Lastly, this point is as straightforward as it sounds.

This is what I mentioned a lot throughout the book. Patience is key. No one can master one trading strategy within one or two days. Every asset in every market goes in a predictable way. There are no identical patterns that appear in any trading chart so that traders can copy their trading/investing decisions. There is no rule written in stone in the financial market. What we've tried to do in coping with unpredictable price actions is to filter only the high probability market signals via different tools and techniques so that we have a higher chance of success when applying them consistently.

This emphasizes the importance of patience in trading. You must be patient and avoid making rushed decisions simply to reach a profit target you pre-set for yourself. Patience means you should start with a suitable crypto and stick with it long enough so you can see how to identify a trade setup, when to enter and exit trades, how to remain disciplined in various circumstances, when to sit on the sideline, and more. Try to make every decision as carefully as you can. If it takes weeks or even months, that's fine. No other timeline is more important than that of your own careful choosing.

You may be asking yourself: how will I know when to make the right choice? The key to this is knowing what isn't a good choice. Once you know how to tell bad decisions from good, figuring out the best possible opportunity will be easier. To achieve this, it's important not to participate in the madness taking place at all times in the markets but to realize that markets are crazy because people are crazy too. We all can lose control on account of emotions, but crypto is sensitive ground, and letting loose with it can really hurt. This is because, let us not forget, crypto may not work as money quite yet, but in every technical respect, it is money. Liquidity is the number one enemy of imprudent investment, so if crypto is readily spendable, that's a liability to keep away from. You'll be tempted to spend, and you'll have a chance to do it, but you must withhold. Your guidance shouldn't be impulsive, but the plan you drew way back when emotions were the last thing in your mind.

I'm afraid most tips of this sort don't ever make it through to their audience because crypto is still fairly new. If you're reading this it's probably because you are new to crypto. You're curious about it and can't wait to dip your toes into the pond. In other words, you're anxious. If this description fits your current state of mind, I personally wouldn't advise you to start investing just yet. Anxiety can only push you in the wrong direction. You'll be telling yourself you took all necessary measures, but it'd be more accurate to say that you're just looking for a pretext to spend and see what happens. That's a good way to lose money, so it's no way to invest.

I suggest two options to get past this state of mind. The first one is to take a cold shower, stick to the 1% rule during the beginning of your trading/investing career and constantly remind yourself: No matter what the outcome, this is my monthly allowance, and I must not give myself permission to exceed it. That's the rule, and you must be vigilant about it. If it works right away, you'll find that it's a good method to get the first taste and even make some mistakes without having to worry about gigantic consequences down the line.

The second option is to filter out all rushed decisions to make room for responsible investing. If you find yourself wanting to put money on an obscure ICO because you "heard good things about it," that's your red flag right there. It may well be that the ICO is reliable or even profitable, but that's not the point. You should only invest in things you researched for yourself, things whose background and profitability have been carefully assessed by you. Everything else is just gambling, and you're an investor, not a player.

*

These are some of the ways in which you can hedge against unforeseen situations and volatility-related risk. They all have a common premise: Crypto is volatile, and you must prevent losses from getting out of control. As I said, risk management is important to keep performance at a good level. It shouldn't ever be the center of all your investment activities, but it is undoubtedly a core ingredient.

Crypto is a whole new asset class, and has its own rules, but from a strict investment standpoint, it isn't all that unique or different. The same principles you would apply elsewhere are valid for it, too. You just need to know how to adapt them appropriately. This can be difficult to do when you think how young crypto still is, but if we aim at stepping on solid ground, we simply must take the time and assess all available risk management options.

When something is this new and trendy, uncertainty about it will be on everyone's lips. So day in and day out, you may find yourself submerged in public debate. This sort of environment can alter your emotions and ultimately your investing discipline, regardless of whether you notice it or are willing to admit it. You mustn't think you're invincible because it would be a comforting belief but also an inaccurate one.

The truth of the matter is that when it comes to crypto, we are all facing a still unknown and unpredictable situation. As I said before, we must treat it with respect and pay close attention to the facts. Especially in these times (2021), high inflation will certainly draw a lot of people toward crypto. I already told you what that entails: the cup of coffee will be filled to capacity and beyond. This, in turn, will affect prices, so there will be many opportunities for you to benefit from price shifts, perform successful short-selling ventures, and other options. All of this, though, is not to say that you should sail with a careless attitude. Be alert and do your due diligence of researching before taking any action. That way, your win rate will improve dramatically, and you'll make the most out of this promising time we're about to enter in the world of crypto.

What Is Next?

This brings us to the end of the book.

First of all, I would like to congratulate you for completing these chapters on cryptocurrency trading and investing. If you made it to this section, you are one step closer to taking your trading results to the next level.

By the way, if you find you have learned something useful via this book, please consider leaving an honest review in the review section. I would be very grateful to you.

My Best Always!

Frank Miller.

Check Out Other Books

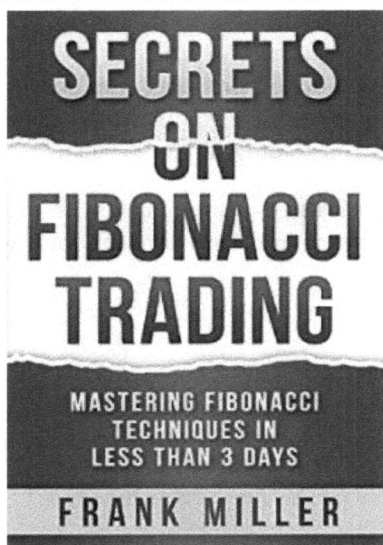

Scan this barcode with your phone camera to check out my No.1 book on Fibonacci trading.

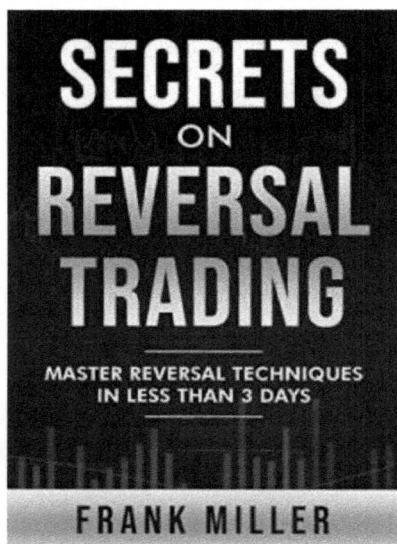

Scan this barcode with your phone camera to check out my No.1 book on reversal trading techniques.

Scan this barcode with your phone camera to learn about the art of trading adopted by BIG PLAYERS in the market.

Scan this barcode with your phone camera to check out a professionally designed trading journal and master discipline in trading.

References

Kenneth, F. (2021, September 13). An Introduction to Bitcoin, Cryptocurrencies and Altcoins. Linkedin. https://www.linkedin.com/pulse/introduction-bitcoin-cryptocurrencies-altcoins-kenneth-fax

Conway, L. (2021, November 29). Bitcoin Halving. Investopedia. https://www.investopedia.com/bitcoin-halving-4843769

(2021, December 17). Why Trade Cryptocurrencies? Exploring the crypto benefits. Altrady. https://www.altrady.com/blog/why-use-cryptocurrency

Khojikian, G. (2021, June 17). The Biggest Risks Of Investing In Bitcoin. Forbes. https://www.forbes.com/sites/forbesbusinesscouncil/2021/06/17/the-biggest-risks-of-investing-in-bitcoin/?sh=b55246c4afd1

Lancette-Smit, M. (2021, April 21). Crypto Tax around the World. Taxably. https://www.taxably.com.au/post/crypto-tax-around-the-world

(2021, August 5). 5 reasons why you should invest in cryptocurrency. Pulse. https://www.pulse.ng/business/5-reasons-why-you-should-invest-in-cryptocurrency/gmvc7zy

(2021, July 23). Cryptocurrency Terms: 60 Terms You Must Know Before Trading. Trading-education. https://trading-education.com/cryptocurrency-terms-60-terms-you-must-know-before-trading

(2021, December 17). Bitcoin Wallets - Become An Expert. Altrady. https://www.altrady.com/blog/bitcoin-wallet

Voigt, K. Rosen, A. (2021, December 21). How to Buy Bitcoin. NerdWallet. https://www.nerdwallet.com/article/investing/how-to-invest-in-bitcoin

Houston, R. The best cryptocurrency exchanges for trading bitcoin and other assets. Businessinsider. https://www.businessinsider.com/personal-finance/best-crypto-bitcoin-exchanges

Can You Trade Cryptocurrencies Using a Forex or CFD Platform? Plus500. https://www.plus500.com/en-US/Trading/CryptoCurrencies/Can-You-Trade-Cryptocurrencies-Using-a-Forex-or-CFD-Platform~5

(2021, July 6). The Best Brokers for Crypto Trading in 2021. Topratedforexbrokers. https://www.topratedforexbrokers.com/cryptocurrency/

What Is Cryptocurrency Leverage Trading And The Risks That Come With It. Thecryptoassociate. https://www.thecryptoassociate.com/what-is-cryptocurrency-leverage-trading-and-the-risks-that-come-with-it/

(2020, July 2). How to Trade Spot on Binance Website. Binance. https://www.binance.com/en/support/faq/115003765031

(2021, June 16). How to Analyze a Cryptocurrency Using Fundamental Analysis. Bybit. https://learn.bybit.com/investing/how-to-analyze-a-cryptocurrency-using-fundamental-analysis/

(2021, June 30). Why Is It Important to Understand Crypto Market Sentiment? Bybit. https://learn.bybit.com/trading/what-is-crypto-market-sentiment/

(2021, June 28). Why Is Technical Analysis Important to Trade Bitcoin? Bybit. https://learn.bybit.com/trading/what-is-technical-analysis/

The law of probability in trading – Trading Secrets. Excellenceassured. https://excellenceassured.com/8225/law-probability-trading

Bohen, T. K.I.S.S.: Why Good Trading Is Simple (and How to Keep It That Way). Stockstotrade. https://stockstotrade.com/k-i-s-s-why-good-trading-is-simple/

Burns, B. (2016, March 26). Why You Should Trade with the Trend. Dummies. https://www.dummies.com/personal-finance/investing/why-you-should-trade-with-the-trend/

(2021, July 05). How to Use Elliott Wave Theory to Spot Crypto Trend. Bybit.
https://learn.bybit.com/trading/using-elliott-wave-theory-to-spot-crypto-trend/

What is Bitcoin Dominance? Cryptocurrencyfacts.
https://cryptocurrencyfacts.com/what-is-bitcoin-dominance/

(2020, March 26). The Relationship Between Altcoins and Bitcoin (Simple). Cryptocurrencyfacts.
https://cryptocurrencyfacts.com/2017/12/15/the-relationship-between-altcoins-and-bitcoin-simple/

Chen, J. (2021, August 25). Support (Support Level). Investopedia.
https://www.investopedia.com/terms/s/support.asp

Chen, J. (2021, July 14). Resistance (Resistance Level) Definition. Investopedia.
https://www.investopedia.com/terms/r/resistance.asp

Chen, J. (2021, August 19). Trendline. Investopedia.
https://www.investopedia.com/terms/t/trendline.asp

How to Trade the Pennant, Triangle, Wedge, and Flag Chart Patterns. Forexschoolonline.
https://www.forexschoolonline.com/pennant-triangle-wedge-and-flag-chart-patterns/

Mitchell, C. (2021, October 30). Rectangle. Investopedia.
https://www.investopedia.com/terms/r/rectangle.asp

Relative Strength Index (RSI). Coinmarketcap.
https://coinmarketcap.com/alexandria/glossary/relative-strength-index-rsi

Regular Divergence. Babypips.
https://www.babypips.com/learn/forex/regular-divergence

Hidden Divergence. Babypips.
https://www.babypips.com/learn/forex/hidden-divergence

Palovaara, A. (2020, May 26), Best Exchanges to Short Crypto in 2021. Tradingbrowser.
https://tradingbrowser.com/best-exchange-to-short-crypto/

www.ingramcontent.com/pod-product-compliance
Lightning Source LLC
Chambersburg PA
CBHW071553210326
41597CB00019B/3228